Middle School in the Making

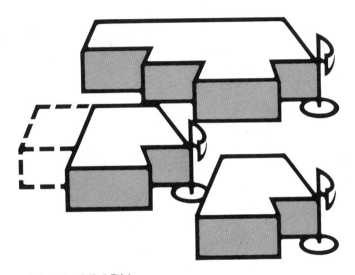

*Readings
from
EDUCATIONAL LEADERSHIP*

Edited by
Robert R. Leeper

Introduction by
William M. Alexander

Association for Supervision and Curriculum Development
1701 K Street, N.W., Washington, D. C. 20006

Stock Number: 611-74024
ISBN 0-87120-042-2

The materials printed herein are the expressions of the writers and not necessarily a statement of policy of the Association.

Library of Congress Catalog Card Number: 74-25223

Second Edition, reprinted November 1975

ACKNOWLEDGMENTS

Special acknowledgment is made to the authors for permission to reprint the articles appearing in this book of readings. Robert R. Leeper, Associate Director and Editor, ASCD publications, was responsible for final editing and production of the selections. Technical production was handled by Nancy Olson, Elsa Angell, Maureen Montgomery, and Teola T. Jones, with Caroline Grills as production manager. Cover design by McMeans Graphics.

Contents

Foreword

The Middle School:
A Significant Mutation

Robert R. Leeper

ONE occupational hazard—and reward—of school work is the necessity to recognize, to accept, and to help shape *change*. Education is susceptible to change, and, indeed, should welcome change, for to adapt to the varying demands of the times is a mandatory and most difficult function of schooling.

Persons in school work are sometimes able to distinguish an important, definite, and significant change. Such a mutation seems to have developed in recent years in the organizational structure of the school. This variation in structure relates to the change of critical interest and support from the traditional junior high school organization and program to a newer structure and approach advocated in the middle school movement.

The traditional junior high school organization and program have for some years caused much concern. This level of schooling has seemed to some to be too much influenced by the high school curriculum and thereby not adequately to have met the needs of the junior high school aged learner. The earlier maturation rate of today's youngsters has also stimulated much recent and current thought and research at this level of schooling.

Observation of and experience with sixth graders suggest that they are more compatible with seventh and eighth graders than with upper elementary children. Moreover, the maturity of ninth graders seems much more compatible with that of high school students than with seventh and eighth grade youngsters. In addition, the ninth grade program appears to resemble more closely the high school program; for example, the computation of Carnegie units begins at this level. Such indications seem to reinforce the need for critical attention to needed adaptations in structure, program, staff, and facilities at this transitional level of schooling. Out of such concern and interest has emerged the impressive and burgeoning middle school movement.

Most of the 32 articles in this book of selected readings appeared in the Decem-

Foreword • v

ber 1973 issue of *Educational Leadership,* on the theme, "Middle School in the Making?" Several of the contributions appeared in earlier issues of the journal, and are included here as representing important harbingers of this important curricular and organizational adjustment.

Rich Resources Are Available

Included herein also are four new and original contributions to the volume, the introduction by William M. Alexander; an article prepared by Conrad F. Toepfer entitled, "Curriculum Planning Priorities for the Middle School"; "Programs for Emerging Adolescent Learners," written by Joseph C. Bondi, Jr., for the ASCD Working Group on the Middle School and the Emerging Adolescent Learner; and "Middle School Research 1968-1974: A Review of Substantial Studies," by Jon W. Wiles and Julia Thomason. We felt that the first statement was needed to place the middle school movement within the broader perspective of historical change in education. The second statement was requested as a means of distilling and expressing in a single source some of the rich and multifaceted elements now increasingly utilized in the curricular resources of the middle school. The third statement demonstrates the continuing commitment of ASCD in the ongoing development of the middle school. The fourth article is an update on the significant research being conducted on the middle school.

Contributions to this volume are presented in five sections:

1. Why the Middle School? Rationale
2. The Middle School: What Is It?
3. Middle Schoolers and Their Teachers
4. Curriculum for the Middle School
5. Middle Schools in Action.

The reader is invited to explore further the writings of many of the outstanding contributors to this work. Additional authors and resources are frequently referred to in the following pages and may be used to round out the full picture of the promise, the problems, the structure, and the program of the middle school. Even a cursory examination will reveal that this field is a new and open one, with a growing body of literature and other supportive resources.

The decision to publish this book of readings was based upon the instant and almost unprecedented demand for additional copies of the December 1973 issue of *Educational Leadership* following its distribution to members and subscribers. This demand seems to have continued, as evidenced by many orders and inquiries. Because the Association must be vigilant in meeting the needs and concerns of its constituencies, serious notice has been taken of these signs of continuing interest in the middle school area. As a result this anthology is offered as one means of furthering interest in, and an understanding of, this significant development in the structure and program of this segment of the common school.

We express our gratitude to all the contributors to this anthology who have consented to this further usage of their material. We are especially appreciative of the cooperation of Dr. Alexander, Dr. Toepfer, Dr. Bondi, Dr. Wiles, and Ms. Thomason for their generous response to our expression of need.

Special acknowledgment is also due to Maurice R. Ahrens, Professor Emeritus, University of Florida, Gainesville, who, as a member of the ASCD Publications Committee, drew up the original plan for the December 1973 issue of *Educational Leadership* on "Middle School in the Making?"

Ours is a time of change in education. This volume will help the reader to define the need and to understand the potential structure and program for such change in a new and significant area of schooling.

—ROBERT R. LEEPER, *Associate Director and Editor, Association for Supervision and Curriculum Development.*

Introduction

The Middle School Emerges

William M. Alexander

WATCHING, even abetting, the emergence of the new middle school since 1960 has been interesting indeed. We may be witnessing a long needed resolution of the dilemmas created by the graded school ladder and its various rungs and levels. Confused as the middle school movement has been by continuing controversies and uncertainties about grade organizations, enrollment and building problems, and desegregation plans, its focus on the transition from childhood to adolescence gives the movement validity and significance. This new volume of the Association for Supervision and Curriculum Development is welcomed as evidence both of the widespread interest in the middle school and of the commitment of ASCD to its continuing emergence as a significant phase of American education.

Burgeoning in numbers only recently, today's model of a really transitional middle school has been long in the making. Its origins are inextricably related to those of the junior high school it is replacing, or perhaps reforming. Although the junior high

school was first proposed at the turn of the century, as a means of extending secondary education downward, and this goal it achieved all too well, it, too, was seen by many as a transitional or bridge school. Usually classified, staffed, scheduled, and programmed as a secondary school, however, the junior high school tended to neglect the bridging function and herein arose the demands for its reform or replacement. But not all junior high, intermediate, or upper elementary schools, as they were variously called, were modeled after the high school, and it was in the more transitional models that many features of the middle school developed. For example, long before the current middle school movement, the Skokie Junior High School of the Winnetka, Illinois, Elementary School District enrolled children in grades 6-8, provided "survey" or short-term exploratory courses, utilized team teaching and modular scheduling, had student "enterprises" as special interest activities, and featured individualized instruction using materials developed within the school organization. Such schools were relatively few in number but their programs were forerunners of many emergent middle schools of the current decade.

Focus on the Transitional Years

In the early 1960's mounting dissatisfaction with the discontinuity of elementary and secondary schools and the resultant problems of children in moving from level to level, along with widespread criticism of schooling in general, and the search for innovations and alternatives created a receptive climate for middle school proposals and reorganizations. My 1968 survey identified 1101 middle schools, classified on the basis of grade organization, which was more than twice the number William Cuff had identified two years earlier and less than half the number Ronald Kealy was to identify two years later. One guesses from local and state reports that the number may have doubled again, perhaps to some 4,000, in 1974, although there is no comparable survey available. But the more significant development, in my opinion, is the evidence from the literature and from firsthand contact with many middle schools that the movement today is more than the grade reorganization it tended to be in 1968—that the true focus of the middle school on the transitional years is catching on and being reflected in practice.

The power of the middle school movement may lie in the lack of uniformity of the new organizations. Although one can be dismayed by the evidence that many so-called middle schools are really traditional junior high schools with only the grades included changed, one can also be pleased by the evidence elsewhere of local invention and experimentation with new and exciting practices. Should forces of accreditation and standardization bring about uniformity as to the grades included, the program offered, the instructional organization and system, and the physical facilities, the middle school also may in time become institutionalized, obsolescent, and a target for reform. As of today, the new middle school, being less

hampered by tradition and standardization, offers educators and their communities an attractive opportunity to create educational structures and processes adapted to present needs and adaptable for future ones.

There are, of course, some central guidelines which each local planning group may need to consider in developing the program and structure to meet its educational priorities. The first of these relates to the planning process itself. Too many reorganized middle schools were created out of expediency without a carefully developed plan—these in general are the schools that changed only the grades included. Fortunately many schools so created have become or are becoming good middle schools because planning followed the reorganization it would have more logically and easily preceded.

Ideas To Be Considered

The articles in this volume suggest many ideas to be considered in the establishment of middle school planning processes. The following deserve special emphasis:

1. As a critical link in the chain of continuous progress education, the middle school should be planned with full consideration of the levels it bridges. Planning groups should represent the entire chain of elementary–middle–high school education.

2. In view of the critical need for parental and general community assistance in the development and operation of the middle school, as early and full participation as possible should be sought.

3. The total range of planning—goal setting, curriculum designing, curriculum implementation, and evaluation, with adequate opportunity for feedback in each phase —should be anticipated in setting up the planning mechanisms. Time schedules for preliminary plans, planning processes prior to school opening, and planning processes during operation, are needed.

Another set of guidelines has to do with the goals of the new middle school. Clearly these goals must be related to the particular educational needs of an age population in transition from childhood to adolescence. Articles in this volume and elsewhere identify many of these needs, and local planning groups should be expected to interpret the research and literature in terms of their own children and community.

The critical guideline is for the planning groups and the operational staffs to recognize fully the transitional nature of the middle school and its population and to provide the wide variety of programs and services needed to match the highly variable and changing characteristics of children in the middle. It is in its range of individual differences that the middle school has a measure of uniqueness and a corresponding justification and challenge. Because of the facts of its population, the middle school should be expected to give special emphasis to programs and services serving the personal development needs of the "tweenager." And it is here too that curriculum plans reflecting continuums of objectives, skills, and concepts become particularly critical so that students at widely varying entry points on the continuums may be helped to move forward smoothly and successfully.

A third set of central guidelines relates to the staff of the middle school. Teacher education institutions are in the early stages of developing preservice programs. Many types of in-service programs of varying quality are being utilized. Needed teacher competencies have been identified in part, and training programs may well reflect these more fully in the future. Undoubtedly continued research and experimentation will help to provide more middle school personnel sympathetic to the goals of the movement, competent and interested in working with middle school children, and committed to the continuous progress education which the middle school is intended to facilitate. The need for such personnel is indeed urgent.

What Is Needed?

What then has been accomplished by the middle school movement as of 1975, and what may be ahead for it? In general, I believe we may feel encouraged about the past 15 years of middle school development and optimistic about its future. True, some middle schools are not significantly different from or better than their predecessor organizations; neither are they worse. Many of these and other middle schools are valiantly trying to achieve the promise of the movement—to become better schools for children in transition from childhood to adolescence, and thereby to tie together better the entire program of schooling through the high school. And still other middle schools, increasing in number, are really demonstrating the qualities and the successes that we have dreamed about. Research evidence is scant, as it has been for other forms of educational organization, but it seems favorable in results and growing in quantity.

What is needed ahead includes careful study of such sources as are contained in this volume, informed and purposeful planning and evaluation of more and more middle schools, development of more and better personnel training programs, and continued exploration, evaluation, and support of the movement by the profession and by local communities. With these steps, I believe that the middle school movement will survive and indeed strengthen schooling by helping it become a successful forward incline toward continued learning for every student. The Association for Supervision and Curriculum Development and the authors of these articles give the movement further impetus by this publication.

—WILLIAM M. ALEXANDER, *Professor of Education, University of Florida, Gainesville.*

PART 1

Why the Middle School? Rationale

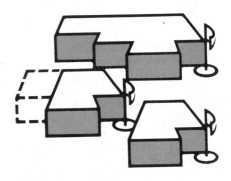

EL 31 (3): 195-97; December 1973
© 1973 ASCD

Middle School in the Making

Donald H. Eichhorn

RECENTLY I visited the Lounsberry Hollow Middle School in New Jersey. As I talked casually with students and teachers, it seemed to me that a feeling of excitement and enthusiasm permeated the entire school. One student responded to the inevitable question of how she liked her school with this brief but descriptive reply, "It is really neat." Her response seemed to sum up the feeling I have sensed among transescents and adults in so many middle schools which I have been privileged to visit throughout the nation.

It was the same feeling I experienced as I listened to a faculty team leader from the Rupert Nock Middle School in Newburyport, Massachusetts, as he told me of his joy in teaching in the middle school. It was the same feeling I received from an urban principal in Detroit, Michigan, as he described the favorable change in student and teacher attitude at the recently implemented Pelham Middle School. It occurred to me that, after many years of commitment to the belief that schools in the middle could be exciting, dynamic, and effective, this concept was beginning to come of age.

Since the early 1960's when pioneer schools in Centerville, Ohio; Barrington, Illinois; Eagle Grove, Iowa; Mt. Kisco, New York; and Upper St. Clair, Pennsylvania, suddenly emerged, there has been much discussion regarding the middle school. Many educators have described this movement as a new concept. Rather, I suggest it is a 70-year-old concept rededicated to its basic principles. Certainly, the fundamental idea that this should be a school designed for youngsters in transition from childhood to adolescence is just as accurate today as it was in the early decades of this century. Outstanding schools, whether they are junior high or middle schools, have one common element: a program uniquely designed for the transescent learner.

The middle school movement has emerged rapidly. As more and more middle schools are organized and implemented, some educators express the belief that the middle school movement is simply a convenient excuse to erect new buildings or to achieve racial balance. Others insist that concern for age characteristics is the chief factor responsible for change.

Realistically, all of these various opinions have validity. The impetus for widespread reorganization of any institution in our society rarely can be attributed to a single or even a few causal factors. The mushrooming reorganization of middle schools is no exception. There are at least three significant forces motivating efforts of educators to redefine the function of schools in the middle.

1. There is a growing body of knowledge relating to the characteristics of boys and girls in late childhood and early adolescence that is causing a reaffirmation of the principle of uniqueness espoused by early junior high leaders. The fact that biological maturation is occurring at an earlier age adds to its impact.

2. There are significant changes in our culture such as population shifts, population mobility, the dream of racial equality, developments in transportation and communication, and the forces involved in a developing technology which are prompting a reconsideration of school building as well as organizational pattern.

3. There is a growing realization that schools in the middle have become rigid and institutionalized. A variety of developing educational concepts such as continuous learner progress, flexible schedules, nongrading, interdiscipline curriculum, cooperative planning and teaching, and affective programs appear more likely to succeed in a revised framework.

Current Status

There is considerable difficulty in assessing status or evaluating effectiveness of a movement as complex and recent as the middle school. Limited research results have been encouraging; however, the results have not supported the excessive claims made by many advocates. Personal observation of numerous middle schools provides the impression that schools which have been carefully planned and designed by committed teachers have been quite successful; conversely, those schools hurriedly planned and implemented with little concern for age characteristics or program appear as "changes in name" only.

It is difficult to generalize in this sense; nevertheless, it is impressive to note the growing number of successful middle schools in urban areas such as Detroit, Michigan; Philadelphia, Pennsylvania; Fort Worth, Texas; and Decatur, Alabama. Similarly, one can report many effective suburban middle schools exemplified by those located in Howard County, Maryland; Upper St. Clair, Pennsylvania; and Jamesville-DeWitt, New York. While these are just a few examples of successful middle schools found in vastly different socioeconomic areas, I believe it does confirm the point that effective middle school education can be more than mere speculation.

Despite the paucity of statistical evidence regarding middle school effectiveness, there have been a number of positive outcomes which can be cited. In this regard, the middle school movement has:

• Prompted a reconsideration of the purpose and programs for the transescent learner

• Provided our society with a means to adjust to the pluralistic needs of its citizenry

• Enabled teachers to emphasize learners rather than structure

• Pioneered organization and learning strategies

• Caused state departments of education, universities, and the public to reassess basic positions

• Reaffirmed the concept that a unique level of education exists between the elementary and high school levels

• Provided a catalyst for change and articulation of the total K-12 program

• Established a convenient vehicle for the employment of promising instructional concepts such as open education, continuous learner progress, and nongrading

• Created opportunities for educational alternatives within the public school system

• Provided potential for future growth and development.

The middle school is "in the making." In many respects, this movement might be compared to the mercurial nature of the transescent. The movement is replete with a growing enthusiasm, interest, desire to achieve, and a quest for a favorable self-concept. In a substantive way, this movement has provided a fresh opportunity for concerned educators to create appropriate programs for the transescent learner. In addition, a dynamic instructional format, which encourages diversity and change rather than standardization and rigidity, is evolving.

If the middle school movement is to achieve its great potential, there is an urgent need for support from all facets of the educational establishment. It is time for the leadership of the great associations such as the National Association of Secondary School Principals, the Association for Supervision and Curriculum Development, the National Association of Elementary School Principals, and all associations and agencies with a concern for middle level education to create "an interdisciplinary team" to ensure that transescents benefit from the most enlightened educational program possible. Also, there is an urgent need for teacher education institutions to develop a preparation component emphasizing emerging adolescent education. This preparation strand, if made part of an effective coalition with community, school personnel, and students, could result in a trained group of professionals dedicated to improvement of middle unit education. This cooperation is even more essential if education is to continue to develop in the sensible direction of a continuum of learning experiences rather than the past fragmented format of elementary and secondary divisions.

Vars, in an editorial in *Educational Leadership*, December 1965, offered a thoughtful admonition. His counsel is an appropriate introduction to this issue. He wrote:

Junior high schools are changing. Yet the basic question remains the same. What shall be the nature of education for young adolescents in today's society? Neither changing the institution's name nor moving its grade level brackets up or down a notch will necessarily affect the character of the education it provides. Instead, educators at all levels must seize the opportunity represented by the present state of flux to try once again to make of the intermediate unit a truly unique institution for the age group it embraces.[1]

The guidance embodied in Vars' statement is still applicable today; however, much progress has been made since 1965. I believe this progress will accelerate rapidly in the next few years as a growing number of dedicated professionals are determined to create learning programs which are as exciting and dynamic as the transescents for whom they are intended.

—DONALD H. EICHHORN, *Assistant Superintendent, Upper St. Clair Public Schools, Pennsylvania.*

[1] Gordon F. Vars. "Change—and the Junior High School." *Educational Leadership* 23 (3): 189; December 1965.

The Rouse Co., Columbia, Maryland

EL 31 (3): 242-44; December 1973
© 1973 ASCD

Middle School:

FOR the past two decades the education of the 11- to 14-year-old age group has faced a change. The middle school movement has become a fact, and its initial stage of faddism is over. Or is it?

Middle schools are now the "in thing" in education. The foundations established for the middle schools by Eichhorn, Alexander, and Murphy point to the development of a separate educational structure for this age group. Middle schools are child centered, not subject centered. However, in the transition from the junior high school to the middle school, strange things are happening.

Faced with overcrowded conditions, many districts have found it very convenient to change the grade organization from a 7-8-9 junior high school to a 6-7-8 junior high/ middle school. The trappings of the junior high school remain, and only the name is changed to give an air of respectable innovation to the school. Hence, the middle school becomes a fad and not a fact.

A Lack of Commitment

There are several reasons for this failure on the part of the middle school to become a fact. One could plead that it is a new movement and that not enough is known about the concept to implement it fully. One

could plead that the time is not right for change, that the pendulum is swinging back from the numerous innovations that education has witnessed over the past two decades, and that the social community will not allow such change. One could advance the idea that teacher education has not kept pace with the newer advances inherent in the middle school concept.

All of these reasons may be true, either partially or wholly. However, one important reason needs to be considered when we talk of the failure of the transition from a junior high to a middle school; it is the lack of total commitment on the part of those persons who work most closely with the program. How can this lack of commitment be overcome?

There is need to retrain the staff of the school to enable them to develop self-commitment so that this transition can occur effectively and efficiently. The gradualism that pervades many of the districts that try to move to a middle school affords the opportunity for the continuation of their present program. Attrition of personnel is so slow that it results in the replacement of personnel, but not ideas and concepts. Business and industry have established the precedent for the retraining of their personnel in new methods, concepts, ideas, and skills to keep them current with the present-day business

Fantasy, Fad, or Fact?

GROVER H. BALDWIN*

What is needed for the child of 11 to 14 is not a renamed administrative unit, but a middle school that will allow for his total development both intellectually and socially.

and industry scene. Why not do this on a regular, well-planned basis for education?

Graduate study too often falls within the realm of specialized subject areas and does not prepare a staff for a total change to a new idea. What is needed is a thorough in-service program that will develop understanding and a sense of security in the concepts, ideas, and skills that are inherent within the middle school movement. This will enable the staff to become committed to the middle school movement, allowing for a total transition from the junior high school.

The concepts that are needed are those dealing with the psychology of the pre-adolescent, how he learns, explores, achieves, and grows. The concept of the child-centered approach to education, an approach found in elementary programs but foreign to most subject-centered secondary teachers, needs to be examined and taken to heart. The idea of the child doing the learning in an active environment that allows him to explore, touch, feel, and accept and/or

reject ideas based on his needs and decisions is quite different from the dispensing of information by the lecture/recitation methods traditionally used within junior and senior high schools. The concepts of interpersonal relations and the child's relationship to himself, his fellow classmates, his environment, and the society within which he finds himself must be understood, so that the staff realizes that education is more than mere information processing.

Teachers Need Reorientation

Beyond these concepts, certain skills need to be developed within the staff. These skills are ones that, when mastered, will give the staff member a sense of security in a new role, and will enable him to become committed to the place and function of the middle school in the child's life. These new skills include diagnosis of learning and social disorders and how to deal with them; the various approaches to independent study; the skills inherent in large- and small-group instruction; the skills (mostly human relations) that are part of team teaching; the many facets of

* Grover H. Baldwin, former Middle School Teacher and Administrator, presently completing doctoral studies` at Lehigh University, Bethlehem, Pennsylvania

interdisciplinary team teaching; the concepts and skills that are needed to develop a core type approach to education; the various skills necessary to allow for nongradedness; the skills involved with individualized instruction; and the skills of evaluation, not just of information consumed by the student, but of his attitude and feelings, the aspects of education that deal with his self-concept.

Teachers have been taught by the lecture/recitation method and for most this is the only working model with which they have had contact. It is not a general rule that the teacher is the facilitator of learning, even though we talk a great deal about this concept in education. However, if a true middle school is to evolve from the transition, then the facilitation of education for the 11- to 14-year-old must be the focal point rather than the traditional methods of teaching that are employed today.

The retraining process, with the subsequent development of a commitment to the idea of the middle school, cannot be a hit or miss proposition. It must be a detailed operation from beginning to end. One individual must serve as full-time coordinator for this process, bringing to bear his full talents and resources for the completion of the project. Time-wise this operation must be given at least two years, including summers, to have any real effect in changing attitudes on the part of the staff.

A person who is part of the structure, and not happy, can do more damage than can be overcome by the best concepts and ideas for the child.

In order to accomplish the task, biweekly meetings on the aforementioned topics must be held for the entire staff. These meetings should be an in-depth examination of the positive, as well as the negative, facets of middle school concepts and skills. Everyone should reach a deep understanding of what goes into the makeup of a middle school and how it is to function for the child. In addition to the biweekly meetings, staff members, both individually and in the groups in which they will be working, should be sent to seminars, conferences, and meetings dealing with the middle school so that they can have a feel for the movement and what it can do. Visitations to actively working middle schools, not renamed junior high schools, are of the utmost importance. Change is hard for children, but it is even harder for staff members who are comfortable in old skills and skeptical about new ones.

Actually seeing the concepts work has a vitalizing effect on the needed commitment for this program. This in-service program must be for all members of the staff who intend to become part of the middle school. During the process of change, those who feel that they cannot be comfortable within this structure must be allowed to transfer to another area suitable to their background and social/emotional needs. A person who is part of the structure, and not happy, can do more damage than can be overcome by the best concepts and ideas for the child.

Failure to develop a commitment to the concepts and ideas behind the middle school will lead to failure in the transition. What is needed for the child of 11 to 14 is not a renamed administrative unit, but a middle school that will allow for his total development both intellectually and socially. This transition cannot be a patchwork addition of extras to the program with no basic change within the structure of the curriculum and the organization of the school for the child. This transition cannot occur unless the staff is committed totally to the concepts of the middle school.

From retraining comes commitment and from commitment comes a middle school in fact and not in fad. □

EL 30 (2): 171-74; November 1972
© 1972 ASCD

Middle School Accountability

E. M. TRAUSCHKE*
PATRICK F. MOONEY

LITTLE research is yet available as to the merits of a middle school organization. The "middle school," a hybrid, is emerging as one of the most revolutionary changes in the U.S. public school organization since the establishment of the junior high schools some 60 years ago (5). Critics of the middle school can no longer ignore the fact that the middle school movement is gaining momentum and has validated its existence through recognized channels of accountability.

The term "middle school" means many things to educators and non-educators today. Many definitions of the term are very general, and this leads to misinterpretation and further confusion. The junior high school earlier was vulnerable for this very reason. As Popper stated, "As a first step, let it be clearly marked that no substantive meaning attaches to the name junior high school. The name is an accident of history" (7).

The authors believe that the following characteristics best describe the middle school organization:

1. A middle school takes full cognizance of the dynamic physical, social, and intellectual changes that are occurring in young people during the 10- to 14-year-old age span, and provides a program with the major purpose of creating a facilitative climate so that the transescent (2) can understand himself and the changes that are occurring within and around him.

2. Middle schools generally locate the ninth grade, with the awesome influence of the Carnegie unit, in senior high school settings. The rationale supporting this decision is usually that ninth graders are more like tenth, eleventh, and twelfth grade students than like seventh and eighth grade students.

3. Middle schools provide opportunities for innovation. Such innovations might include team teaching, individualized instruction, flexible scheduling, and some form of continuous progress. Flexible rearrangements of time, space, materials, and people give evidence to the value of the true middle school.

4. Middle schools de-emphasize the sophisticated activities that are commonly found

* E. M. Trauschke, Principal, Miami Edison Middle School, Miami, Florida; and Patrick F. Mooney, Director of Elementary/Secondary Schools, North Central Area, Dade County Public Schools, Miami Springs, Florida

Why the Middle School? Rationale • 9

in the junior high school, such as marching bands, interscholastic athletics, and sophisticated dances. The program of activities which is provided permits each child to participate and is based on the personal development of the student rather than the enhancement of the school's prestige.

5. Middle schools provide opportunities for exploratory study and enrichment activities earlier than do conventional elementary schools.

6. Middle school instructional staffs combine the usual talents developed by teachers trained and oriented in the elementary school with the ability to specialize in a given field, so often a "characteristic" of a secondary teacher.

Middle School Research

Research specificially related to the middle school, as defined by the authors, is extremely limited. There has been little effort on the part of individuals, school systems, or outside agencies to evaluate the middle school. Recently some research studies,

mainly doctoral dissertations, have contributed to a better understanding of the middle school; but in most cases the research leaves unanswered the question of whether or not the middle school is providing a better education for its students than is received by comparable students in the junior high schools.

Mooney (6) and Trauschke (11), at the conclusion of a year's study at the University of Florida as participants in a Middle School Institute, returned to the Dade County, Florida, school system, where they tested several hypotheses in a functioning middle school. Results of these studies are discussed in this article. Miami Edison Middle School was identified as the experimental school for purposes of their studies.

The aged physical plant of the experimental school was not renovated for the conversion to a middle school. Some proponents of the middle school suggest that a middle school and a new physical facility are synonymous. While the middle schools of Centerville, Ohio, and Mount Kisco, New York, are exemplary, they do not provide a model for hard-pressed urban areas where inadequate capital outlay budgets, burgeoning populations, and desegregation demand a reorganization and restructuring of outmoded school practices—especially the questionable use of time, space, personnel, and materials. Creative, relevant, functional use of existing school resources is a challenge of the seventies.

A Study of Achievement

The reorganization of the Miami Edison Middle School was achieved using the same instructional staff allocation as junior high schools in the Dade County school system. The staff was organized into interdisciplinary teams, each team composed of four teachers (math, science, social studies, and language arts). Approximately 140 students were assigned heterogeneously to the team for a five-hour block of time. The block of time permitted flexibility because it enabled the team to group and regroup and to utilize large group and small group instruction.

The extended period also permitted time to provide more appropriate learning opportunities and experiences for the individual child. For example, a child deficient in certain math skills could take more than the 55 minutes per day in math at the discretion of the team. Planning was limited to one hour daily. The team shared a common planning period; unfortunately, a second personal planning period was not provided.

Mooney (6) and Trauschke (11) addressed themselves to the achievement of middle school students in grades 5-6-7-8 when compared with that of students in grades 5 and 6 in elementary and grades 7 and 8 in junior high, using the same control and experimental groups. Student attitudes and self-concepts were also examined to determine the impact of the middle school on the affective dimension of development. Further, these studies compared attendance of middle school students with that of students in conventional school organizations. As a final test, the graduates of the experimental middle school were compared in the ninth grade (four-year senior high setting) to ninth graders in the control 7-8-9 junior high school.

Of the 395 ninth graders enrolled during the 1969-70 school year, 222 former middle school students from Miami Edison Middle School were the subjects of this study. The racial composition of this group was 50 percent Negro, 22 percent of Spanish origin, and 28 percent others.

The three schools used as the control schools were in close proximity to the middle school. The schools were selected after a study of population reports, meetings with representatives of the district office, and the involvement of the research and development section and the testing section of the central county office.

The following five hypotheses were tested:

1. "Achievement of middle school pupils on standardized test scores will equal or exceed that of pupils in elementary and junior high schools." A multiple linear regression—grade, race, and selected subtests of standardized tests —was the method of analysis used. With an experimental population of 1,048 and a control population of 947, comparisons were made. Using the .05 level of significance, 25 null hypotheses were not rejected, indicating no significant difference in achievement. Seven hypotheses indicated greater academic achievement for the students in the middle school when compared to students in the control schools (6).

2. "Middle school graduates will score as high or higher on the ninth-grade standardized test in the senior high setting as the ninth graders in the (control) junior high setting." The statistical treatment for this hypothesis was the same as the treatment used in testing the first hypothesis. With an experimental population of 188 and a control population of 207 and using a covariate IQ, 12 cell comparisons of achievement were made. Nine of the 12 null hypotheses tested were not rejected indicating no significant difference in academic achievement between students in the experimental and control schools. Three null hypotheses indicating greater achievement for students in the experimental school were rejected (6).

3. "The average daily attendance of middle school pupils will be higher than pupil attendance in elementary and junior high schools." Percent of attendance data for seven 20-day reporting periods, September-March, were analyzed by the sign test. Twenty-seven of the 28 comparisons made favored the experimental school. Data were also tested by a multivariate analysis of variance, using the following variables: treatment, grade, and month. Five of the six sources of variance were significant beyond the .01 level (6).

4. "Pupils in the middle school will have more favorable attitudes toward school than will pupils in elementary and junior high schools." Students at each grade level in the middle school were compared with students at each grade level in conventional school using *Battle's Attitude Scale*, which has self factor, fellow following factor, school factor, and teacher-principal factor for purposes of comparison. Of the 30 comparisons there were 21 apparent differences favoring the middle school, and 8 significant differences favoring the middle school (11).

5. "Pupils in the middle school will have more adequate self-concepts than will students in elementary and junior high schools." This was tested using Gordon's *How I See Myself*

Scale, which included the following subtests: teacher-school factor, autonomy factor, peer factor, academic factor, emotions factor, and language adequacy factor. From 60 comparisons there were 28 apparent differences favoring the middle school, and 8 significant differences favoring the middle school. This hypothesis was accepted at the seventh grade level only (11).

Only through systematic long-term study can middle schools throughout the nation prove to be all that middle school proponents claim. Middle schools may overcome the shortcomings of the organizational and program failures of the school organizations which they are replacing; however, provision must be made to assess the effectiveness of ongoing middle schools. Without systematic evaluation we compound the problems prevalent in the elementary and the junior high schools.

School systems must include in their planning for middle schools guidelines for the evaluation of these schools. Unless stated objectives are clearly defined in measurable terms, the middle school movement will continue to be more of the same—schools which purport to change but revert to the familiar, outmoded models from which they departed.

References

1. William M. Alexander, Emmett Williams, Mary Compton, Vynce A. Hines, Dan Prescott, and Ronald Kealy. *The Emergent Middle School.* New York: Holt, Rinehart and Winston, Inc., 1968. pp. 139-45.

2. Donald H. Eichhorn. *The Middle School.* Columbus, Ohio: Center for Applied Research in Education, Inc., 1967. p. 3.

3. Carl H. Glissmeyer. "Which School for the Sixth Grade, the Elementary or Middle School?" *California Journal of Educational Research* 20: 176-85; September 1969.

4. Dale E. Harris. "A Comparative Study of Selected Middle Schools and Selected Junior High Schools." *Dissertation Abstracts* 29: 2924A-25A; February 1969.

5. Ronald P. Kealy. "The Middle School Movement." *The National Elementary Principal* 50: 20-25; November 1971.

6. Patrick F. Mooney. "A Comparison of Achievement and Attendance of 10- to 14-Year-Olds

in a Middle School and in Other School Organizations." Doctoral dissertation, University of Florida, Gainesville, 1970.

7. Samuel H. Popper. *The American Middle School.* Waltham, Massachusetts: Blaisdell Publishing Company, 1967. p. 9.

8. P. Pumerantz *et al.* "A Comparative Study of Self-Perceptions of Middle School and Non-Middle School Pupils." Unpublished study, 1969.

9. William F. Stephens. "A Study of the Relationship Between Self-Concept, IQ, and Reading Comprehension in a Selected Middle School." *Dissertation Abstracts* 30: 2270A; December 1969.

10. Virgil E. Strickland. "Where Does the Ninth Grade Belong?" *NASSP Bulletin* 51: 74-89; February 1967.

11. Edward M. Trauschke. "An Evaluation of a Middle School by a Comparison of the Achievement, Attitudes, and Self-Concept of Students in a Middle School with Students in Other School Organizations." Doctoral dissertation, University of Florida, Gainesville, 1970. □

EL 31 (3): 221-24; December 1973
© 1973 ASCD

Research findings in the middle school to date show a "mixed bag" of results. If some positive trends continue, however, middle schools may yet fulfill their promise.

What Research Says About the Middle School

THOMAS E. GATEWOOD*

DURING its infancy in the early 1960's many of the middle school's early proponents touted its promise. It would be different from the junior high, not only in name and grade organization, but also in the quality of education provided for students. Overcome would be the junior high's weaknesses. Implemented instead would be an educational program focused on the period of growth and development occurring between childhood and adolescence and characterized by:

1. A home base and teacher for every student to provide for continuing guidance and assistance to help him make the decisions he faces almost daily regarding special needs and learning opportunities

2. A program of learning opportunities offering balanced attention to three major goals of the middle school: (a) personal development of the between-ager, (b) skills of continued learning, and (c) effective use of appropriate knowledge

3. An instructional system focused on individual progress, with many curricular options and with individualized instruction in appropriate areas

4. The use of interdisciplinary team ar-

rangements for cooperative planning, instructing, and evaluating

5. A wide range of exploratory activities for the socializing, interest-developing, and leisure-enriching purposes of the bridge school (1).

Yet after a decade of meteoric growth, what has really happened to the original promise of the middle school? What has been learned from the available research?

The following conclusions have emerged from several research studies, many completed only within the past five years.

● *The history of the middle school movement has been characterized by phenomenal emergence of new grade organizations for the middle grades.*

When did you first hear the words, "middle school"? The odds are great that it was not before 1960. A National Education Association survey (29) in 1963-64 found only 20 of 443 school systems reporting schools organized on a grades 5-8 or 6-8 organizational pattern. Only two years later, Cuff (7) identified 449 middle schools (schools

* Thomas E. Gatewood, *Associate Professor of Secondary Education, Central Michigan University, Mount Pleasant*

having grades 6 and 7 and not extending below grade 4 or above grade 8). Of these schools, 35 percent were organized on a grades 6-8 basis, and 30 percent on a 5-8 basis.

In 1967-68, Alexander (2) reported 1,101 middle schools (using a definition similar to Cuff's). Study of a 10 percent random sample of these schools indicated that 60 percent had grades 6-8, 27.4 percent had grades 5-8, and 12.7 percent had either grades 4-8, 5-7, 6-9, or 4-7 organizations.

Kealy (21) found 2,298 middle schools (using Alexander's definition) a year later in 1969-70. The grades 6-8 organization was still most popular, accounting for 58.2 percent of the schools, followed by the 5-8 pattern at 25.4 percent. Thus, during a six-year period, the increase in middle schools was geometric, with the number more than doubling every two years.

● *Middle schools have been established for reasons more administrative than educational.*

As documented by several studies (2, 11, 16, 17, 22, 36, 40), reorganization of the grades in the middle years has been attributed primarily to such practical reasons as to eliminate crowded conditions in other schools, to utilize a new building, to move grade 9 into high school, and to aid desegregation. More strictly educational reasons such as to provide a more appropriate program for pre- and early-adolescent students, to better bridge the elementary school and the high school, and to implement innovative plans for curriculum, instruction, and organizational structure have been less emphasized.

● *Middle schools have adopted the educational programs and practices of junior highs, thus not successfully achieving the middle school concept.*

The junior high versus middle school controversy has existed since the early days of the middle school. Claims and counter-claims have been made, but only recently has research been conducted to determine whether or not differences really exist.

In truth, the only real difference between most junior highs and middle schools is in name and grade organization. Founded more upon grounds of administrative expedience than of educational improvement, most middle schools have simply moved the junior high structure, program, and schedule down a grade or two. Or, the programs of grades 5 and/or 6 from the prior elementary school and that of grades 7 and/or 8 from the junior high are maintained so that, in reality, two very different schools are housed in the same building. Most of the research on the topic (2, 4, 5, 15, 17, 19, 23, 26, 30, 31, 40) reports that middle schools tend to have the same high school-type program of studies, departmental organization, Carnegie units, interscholastic athletics, and early socialization activities that have long characterized and plagued junior highs.

Based upon these findings, it should come as no surprise that several studies (14, 17, 24, 33) have found a significant gap between the main tenets of the theoretical middle school concept proposed by leading middle school authorities and actual educational practices in most middle schools.

Some studies (3, 8, 27, 32, 35, 36, 39) have favored the middle school over the junior high; others (10, 20, 34, 37), the junior high over the middle school. However, many of these studies tend to be either too specific in focus, confined to too small a sample, or too conflicting with one another to be very conclusive.

● *The most appropriate grade organization for the middle school cannot be determined from the available research.*

Do fifth and/or sixth graders belong in an elementary or a middle school? In terms of personal, social, and physical characteristics, research (6, 9) indicates that sixth graders are more like seventh graders than fifth graders. The reason is related to the onset of puberty, which has not begun for most fifth graders as it has for sixth graders. Thus, pupils in the fifth grade still resemble children more than they do early adolescents. Research (12, 13, 25, 36) has reported an age for the onset of puberty approximately one to two years earlier than in preceding generations and an accelerated growth process.

Where should ninth graders be placed?

Ninth graders are more compatible with tenth graders than eighth graders in terms of physical, social (9), emotional, and intellectual (28) maturity.

Based upon the foregoing findings, a grades 6-8 organization would appear to be more appropriate. However, some research (4, 18, 27, 39) reports that it makes no difference to the educational achievement (18), self-concept, attitude toward school (27, 39), and acceptance among peers (4) of fifth and/or sixth grade pupils whether they are placed in either an elementary or a middle school. In addition, none of the studies on grade organization takes into account the obvious differences in maturity between boys and girls. Taking this factor into account, and offering a compromise among the many conflicting studies on grade organization, one perceptive educator was moved to suggest, with tongue only partly in cheek, that the best middle school organization would have all seventh and eighth graders, plus sixth grade girls and ninth grade boys.

The Future of Middle Schools

Despite the disparaging evidence reported in the research, some middle schools are becoming more diverse and innovative in their educational programs. The percentage of schools reporting a variety of the following types of practices appears to be increasing each year: interdisciplinary team teaching; exploratory programs; nongraded and individualized instruction; flexible scheduling; open classrooms; innovative plans for reading instruction; and more personalized guidance services.

The movement toward true middle schools has been given much impetus from new state organizations such as those in Florida, Maryland, and Michigan, and from regional organizations such as the Midwest Middle School Association. New publications such as the *Middle School Journal, Transescence: The Journal on Emerging Adolescent Education*, and *Dissemination Services on the Middle Grades* have emerged to give national identity to the middle school movement. In addition, a plethora of books and articles on the topic have appeared in recent years. More teacher certification is now found at the state level, which in turn has spawned new pre-service training at the college level and in-service training at the school level.

If all of these positive trends continue, research conducted on middle schools in the future hopefully will reveal more fulfillment of their original promise than that conducted to date.

References

1. William M. Alexander. "How Fares the Middle School?" *National Elementary Principal* 51: 8-11; November 1971.

2. William M. Alexander. *A Survey of Organizational Patterns of Reorganized Middle Schools.* Washington, D.C.: U.S. Department of Health, Education, and Welfare, 1968.

3. Fred Baruchin. "A Comparative Study of Transitional Grades of Middle and Traditional School Types in Upstate New York." Unpublished doctoral dissertation, State University of New York at Buffalo, 1971.

4. David A. Case. "A Comparative Study of Fifth Graders in a New York Middle School with Fifth Graders in Elementary Self-Contained Classrooms." Unpublished doctoral dissertation, University of Florida, 1970.

5. Peter S. Constantino. "A Study of Differences Between Middle School and Junior High School Curricula and Teacher-Pupil Classroom Behavior." Unpublished doctoral dissertation, University of Pittsburgh, 1969.

6. Roy J. Creek. "Middle School Rationale: The Sixth Grade Component." Unpublished doctoral dissertation, University of Pittsburgh, 1969.

7. William A. Cuff. "Middle Schools on the March." *National Association of Secondary School Principals Bulletin* 51: 82-86; February 1967.

8. Thomas E. Curtis. "The Middle School in Theory and Practice." *National Association of Secondary School Principals Bulletin* 52: 135-40; May 1968.

9. Wilfred P. Dacus. "A Study of the Grade Organizational Structure of the Junior High School as Measured by Social Maturity and Opposite Sex Choice." Unpublished doctoral dissertation, University of Houston, 1963.

10. Harl R. Douglass. "What Type of Organization of Schools?" *Journal of Secondary Education* 41: 358-64; December 1966.

11. Educational Facilities Laboratories. *The Schoolhouse in the City.* New York: the Laboratories, 1966.

12. Donald H. Eichhorn. *The Middle School.*

New York: Center for Applied Research in Education, 1966.

13. Dorothy H. Eichorn. "Variations in Growth Rate." *Childhood Education* 44: 286-91; January 1968.

14. John H. Flynn. "Practices of the Middle School in California." Unpublished doctoral dissertation, University of Southern California, 1971.

15. Charles F. Forst. "A Study of the Middle Schools in the County School Systems in the State of Maryland as Compared to Selected Junior High Schools Within the State." Unpublished doctoral dissertation, George Washington University, 1969.

16. Alexander Frazier. *The New Elementary School.* Washington, D.C.: Association for Supervision and Curriculum Development, 1968.

17. Thomas E. Gatewood. "A Comparative Study of the Functions, Organizational Structure, and Instructional Process of Selected Junior High Schools and Selected Middle Schools." Unpublished doctoral dissertation, Indiana University, 1970.

18. Carl H. Glissmeyer. "Which School for the Sixth Grader, the Elementary or the Middle School?" *California Journal of Educational Research* 20: 176-85; September 1969.

19. Dale E. Harris. "A Comparative Study of Selected Middle Schools and Selected Junior High Schools." Unpublished doctoral dissertation, Ball State University, 1968.

20. Alvin W. Howard. *Teaching in Middle Schools.* Scranton, Pennsylvania: International Textbook Company, 1968.

21. Ronald D. Kealy. "The Middle School Movement, 1960-70." *National Elementary Principal* 51: 20-25; November 1971.

22. Leslie W. Kindred. *The Intermediate Schools.* Englewood Cliffs, New Jersey: Prentice-Hall, Inc., 1968.

23. Jack E. Kittell. "Changing Patterns of Education: The Middle School Years." *College of Education Record, University of Washington* 33: 62-88; May 1967.

24. Morris Mellinger and John Rackauskas. *Quest for Identity: National Survey of the Middle School, 1969-70.* Chicago: Chicago State College, 1970.

25. Howard V. Meredith. "Change in the Stature and Body Weight of North American Boys in the Last 80 Years." In: Lewis P. Lipsitt and Charles C. Spicker, editors. *Advances in Child Development and Behavior.* New York: Academic Press, 1963.

26. "Middle School Status in Ten States." *National Elementary Principal* 51: 67-77; November 1971.

27. Patrick F. Mooney. "A Comparative Study of Achievement and Attitude of 10- to 14-Year-Olds in a Middle School and in Other School Organiza-

tions." Unpublished doctoral dissertation, University of Florida, 1970.

28. Norman K. Myers. *Physical, Intellectual, Emotional, and Social Maturity Levels of Eighth, Ninth, and Tenth Grade Students with Implications for School Grade Organization.* Columbia: University of Missouri, 1970.

29. National Education Association Research Division. *Middle Schools.* Washington, D.C.: the Association, 1965.

30. National Education Association Research Division. *Middle Schools in Theory and in Fact.* Washington, D.C.: the Association, n.d.

31. John E. Onofrio. "The Evolving Middle School in Connecticut: Principals' Opinions Concerning Unique Characteristics and Recommended Trends." Unpublished doctoral dissertation, Fordham University, 1971.

32. Harold J. Rankin. "A Study of the Pre- and Post-Attitudes and Academic Achievements of Students in Grades 5 through 10 in a Change from a Junior High Organization to a Middle School Organization in a Suburban School System." Unpublished doctoral dissertation, Syracuse University, 1969.

33. Jack Riegle. "A Study of Middle School Programs To Determine the Current Level of Implementation of 18 Basic Middle School Principles." Unpublished doctoral dissertation, Michigan State University, 1971.

34. Charles I. Schonhaut. "An Examination of Educational Research as It Pertains to the Grade Organization for the Middle Schools." Unpublished doctoral dissertation, Columbia University, 1967.

35. Philip H. Schoo. "Students' Self-Concept, Social Behavior, and Attitudes Toward School in Middle and Junior High Schools." Unpublished doctoral dissertation, University of Michigan, 1970.

36. George C. Simpson and George J. Smith. *Middle School Survey of New York State.* New Paltz, N.Y.: Mid-Hudson School Study Council, 1967.

37. Anthony T. Soares, Louise M. Soares, and Philip Pumerantz. "Self-Perceptions of Students in the Middle School." Paper presented at the 1971 Annual Meeting of the American Educational Research Association, New York, 1971.

38. J. M. Tanner. *Education and Physical Growth.* London: University of London Press, 1961.

39. Edward M. Trauschke. "An Evaluation of a Middle School by a Comparison of the Achievement, Attitudes, and Self-Concept of Students in a Middle School with Students in Other School Organizations." Unpublished doctoral dissertation, University of Florida, 1970.

40. George H. Walker, Jr., and Thomas E. Gatewood. "The Status of Middle Schools in Michigan." *Michigan Journal of Secondary Education* 13: 11-15; Summer 1972. ☐

Programs for
Emerging Adolescent Learners

*JOSEPH C. BONDI, JR.**
for the Working Group

IN ITS continuing concern for the emerging adolescent learner, the Association for Supervision and Curriculum Development established a Working Group on the Middle School and the Emerging Adolescent Learner in 1974. The Working Group grew out of a Council on the Emerging Adolescent Learner appointed by ASCD in 1969 and subsequent formal and informal working groups established between 1969 and 1974.

Much progress in American school districts has occurred in the past ten years in developing and implementing new programs for pre- and early adolescents. Middle grades education in many school districts has represented a dramatic break from the past. Building upon growing research on the needs and characteristics of emerging adolescent learners, innovative programs have been developed that include a wide range of learning opportunities for youth in the middle grades. Although many of these programs are housed in new organizational structures called middle schools, such programs can be found in some upper elementary grades as well as in junior high schools and secondary schools. The argument over the name or grade structure of the middle units of schooling has largely disappeared. Perhaps now we are at the point where we can focus on the essence of middle grades education, the emerging adolescent learner group itself.

The Working Group Charge

The ASCD Executive Council in establishing the 1974 Working Group on the Middle School and the Emerging Adolescent

Learner charged the group with the following:

1. That ASCD contact representatives of NASSP, NAESP, and the National Middle School Association in an effort to establish a joint task force. The purpose of this allied effort would be to prepare a working paper dealing with schools for the middle years, stressing guidelines for effective educational programs for these middle years. This working paper would then be presented at the 1975 conference of each of the representative organizations.

2. That a working group be established dealing with the middle years. One of its responsibilities would be to convene a conference of the various regional middle school organizations now operating.

3. That a special session be approved for the 1975 ASCD Annual Conference concerning the middle school years. Providing that the joint task force suggested earlier takes place, the special session would have as one of its aspects a review of the joint position paper.

4. That the working group plan with the national ASCD office staff a National Curriculum Study Institute on Middle School Programs.

In addition to the charge to the Working Group, the ASCD Board of Directors adopted the following position statement:

Teacher Preparation for Middle School Grades Education of Emerging Adolescents

The need to effectively educate emerging adolescent learners in the middle grades continues to receive little specification separate

Joseph C. Bondi, Jr., Associate Professor of Education, University of South Florida, Tampa

from elementary and high school approaches in the majority of American school districts. This need for specification of education in the middle grades requires teacher skills, understandings, and competencies in terms of the nature of the emerging adolescent as a learner and as a total personality. Teacher preparation at both pre- and in-service levels still largely fails to define and offer specific opportunities for teachers in the middle grades by offering such experiences almost exclusively through the foci of elementary and high school concerns. This condition continues to work for the separation and fragmentation of the continuum of the K-12 educational program that is advocated by the Association for Supervision and Curriculum Development.

It is recommended that the ASCD Board of Directors:

1. Take a leadership role in developing a national commitment to the creation of teacher preparation programs with distinct and separate emphases upon defining and/or refining of teacher skills, competencies, and understandings as necessary requisites for improving the quality of the learning experiences for emerging adolescents in the middle grades of the American school system.

2. Utilize its standing Working Groups on the Emerging Adolescent Learner and Teacher Education to facilitate internally these efforts and to initiate dialogue among such organizations as the National TEPS and NCATE toward developing such a commitment.

3. Establish a similar dialogue with state education departments throughout the nation to facilitate their developing regulations for the restructuring of teacher preparation at both pre- and in-service education levels and to provide for this specification within their individual states.

Focusing on the Emerging Adolescent Learner

It has often been repeated that "nothing is so unequal as the equal treatment of unequals." At no time in the schooling of our children do we find greater differences in the physical, social, emotional, and intellectual development of youngsters than during the middle period of ten to fourteen years of age.

The foregoing statement suggests the need for school districts to develop unique school programs for their middle units. It also suggests the need for the establishment of preservice as well as in-service teacher education programs that will prepare teachers to serve emerging adolescent learners. Our public schools cannot continue to accept a "patchwork" preparation that supposedly equips, by the addition of a few extra courses, elementary and high school teachers to teach pre- and early adolescent learners.

Another concern of the Working Group is that school districts in providing unique programs for their middle units plan an articulated K-12 educational program. It is the responsibility of school systems to develop an educational setting that will provide appropriate learning environments for emerging adolescents wherever they appear in the system. We must prepare teachers and staff to work with youngsters whether they reach pubescence at the fourth grade or the tenth grade. We cannot assume that all young people will achieve pubescence coincidentally with the majority of their peers in the middle unit of the school system.

The Role of ASCD

ASCD, through working groups, publications, conferences, institutes, and other leadership activities will involve a broad spectrum of educators at all levels in seeking improved educational opportunities for emerging adolescent learners. The Working Group will fulfill its task only through the cooperation and input of those in the field who share the same concern for the emerging adolescent learner. The help of readers in identifying ways for the Working Group to become more effective as a service component is earnestly solicited.* □

* The ASCD Working Group on the Emerging Adolescent Learner: Joseph C. Bondi, Jr. (Chairman), University of South Florida, Tampa; Robert Bumpus, Decatur, Alabama, City Schools; Charles Dilg, Logansport, Indiana, Community School Corporation; Thomas Gatewood, Central Michigan University, Mt. Pleasant; Inez Wood, Washington, D.C., Public Schools.

PART 2

The Middle School: What Is It?

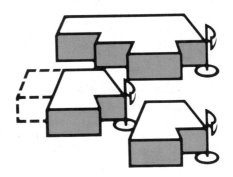

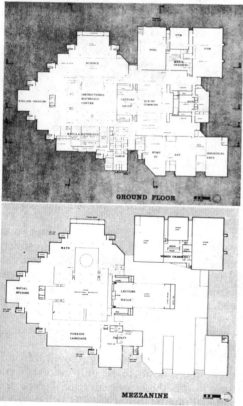

GROUND FLOOR

MEZZANINE

Physical facilities for the middle school should reflect the transition from the self-contained classroom to the mobility of multipurpose flexible spaces, as in these two Connecticut schools, the Avon Middle School (above) and the Branford Intermediate School (three lower photos).

EL 31 (3): 200-205; December 1973
© 1973 ASCD

Purpose and Function Precede Middle School Planning[1]

MICHAEL F. TOBIN*

The middle school facility should represent the flexibility of the program, the rapidly changing child, the motivating atmosphere. It must in itself be a dynamic force, a live and living institution.

MEMBERS of local boards of education, building committees, architects, school superintendents, principals, teachers, and others recently have found themselves involved in the planning, development, and construction of middle schools. It is essential that all persons involved in such endeavors recognize that certain necessary examinations and activities must precede the combining of brick and mortar. The thorough and careful consideration of the purposes and functions of the school will help to assure that the resultant product will be able to best provide that for which it was intended.

How should one go about identifying the purposes and functions of the middle school? High on the list of prerequisites would be achieving an awareness and an understanding of the special characteristics and needs of the students who will be served by such a school. Much overlapping and interrelatedness may exist between and

among the characteristics of this age group. Yet some common traits may be identified according to those which are essentially *physical, social, emotional,* and *intellectual.*

Characteristics and Needs of Middle School Students

Physical—In relation to body development, appearance, and activity, students of middle school age exhibit:

Increased interest in the physical aspects of the body, including its functions and changes

Generally rapid, though irregular, physical development with resultant differences among peers due to uneven growth and development

Generally a more advanced physical maturity on the part of girls than of boys at the same chronological age

[1] This article is based on the Connecticut State Department of Education bulletin, "A Guide to the Writing of Educational Specifications in the Planning of Middle School Programs," of which Dr. Tobin was the principal author. Co-authors with him were John Crawford, Leonard Garber, G. Wesley Ketcham, and Harriet C. Nash, all with the Connecticut State Department of Education.

* *Michael F. Tobin, Consultant for Elementary Education, Connecticut Department of Education, Hartford*

Awkward and clumsy movements due to bone growth preceding muscle growth

Considerable attention to personal appearance and concern with irregularities such as skin blemishes, scars, and obesity

Conformity with "in" styles, such as clothing and hair style

Extreme restlessness with great need to release physical energy

Talkativeness

Responsiveness to a variety of nonstructured and leisure activities.

Social—With their concern for individuality, conformity, and development of values, students of middle school age evidence:

Desire to be "different," yet within the over-all limits of peer conformity

Desire for opportunities to exercise selectivity in the choice of food, activities, and friends—with frequent changes in "close" friendships

Considerable peer consciousness: strong need for a feeling of belonging to a group

Adherence to peer group standards along with awareness of "acceptable behavior"

Concern for "right," "wrong," and "social justice"

Concern for less fortunate "others"

Attempts to identify with adults other than parents.

Emotional—In relation to their uncertainties and conflicts, students of middle school age tend to:

Be frequently impulsive with words and actions; impatient to get things done in a hurry

Have ambivalent desires: want freedom, but fear the loss of certain securities

Become more independent, yet still feel the need for direction and regulation

Desire to make their own evaluation of suggestions from others

Exhibit a wide range of overt behaviors and mood instability: quiet-loud, shy-boisterous, fearful-confident, anxious-assured

Need experience with frequent success and desire attention and recognition for personal efforts and achievements

Seek approval of and acceptance by adults

Learning programs for transescents may utilize multi-age grouping . . .

Be sensitive to criticism of personal shortcomings and often easily offended

Be anxious, doubtful, and confused about their physical and intellectual development, social relationships, and adult authority.

Intellectual—In relation to their intellectual experiences, students of middle school age tend to:

Be curious and inquisitive

Prefer active over passive learning activities

Relate intellectual activities with immediate and short-range goals

Prefer interaction with peers during learning activities

Desire opportunities to express originality on an individual basis

Be interested in both concrete and abstract exercises and be more able to deal with abstract concepts than formerly

Desire opportunities to participate in practical problem-solving situations

Show interest in races and cultures other than their own

Challenge "idealistic" teachings

Be interested in making fuller utilization of basic skills used in the elementary school

Evaluate personal capabilities, both attributes and limitations

Show strong, intense interests, not always sustained, in various pursuits.

Many of the pre- and early-adolescents in the middle school age group will vary in

. . . as well as opportunities for independent work and study.

differing degrees from these generalizations. The major planning direction, however, should be toward providing for both the general and individual needs of the students to be served by the school.

Purposes and Functions

If the general and specific characteristics of the students in the middle school age group are to be the bases for the planning and development of a realistic program, the suggested purposes and functions of the middle school would include the following:

• To provide a program for pre- and early-adolescents that is *relevant* to *individual needs* and *societal demands* in a world where there is constant change and a rapidly expanding body of knowledge. Such a program would consciously aim toward the continuing development of self-directing individuals, capable of solving problems through both rational and creative endeavors.

• To provide an educational environment where the *child* is most important and has opportunities for success. Such an environment would facilitate communication and interaction and afford opportunities for meeting interpersonal needs.

• To provide *orientation* to and *exploration* of the broad spectrum of educational experiences in the world of work, living, and leisure.

• To provide for a *transitional period* of continuous adjustment between the elementary school and the senior high school. This would include emphasis upon a continuation and enrichment of basic education in the concepts and skills pertinent to the general education of the pupil.

• To provide more adequately for *guidance* and *counseling* through the provision of special services and personnel. Aptitudes, interests, and capacities of individual pupils would be discovered by testing, counseling, and exploratory work.

Planning for Learning

The middle school program should be tailored to the needs, interests, and abilities of the child. The primary objective is the motivation to learn and the awareness of the various methods of learning, rather than the mere acquisition of knowledge. The essential skills, understandings, and attitudes to be acquired within each discipline, as well as between and among disciplines, must be carefully defined within the framework of this objective.

The Program. The program for learning in the middle school must give each child opportunities for increasing self-identity, for comprehension of his environment, and attaining his or her full potential in understandings and skills. Development goals include improvements in rational thinking procedures and increased competency in identifying, analyzing, classifying, manipulating, measuring, listening, viewing, communicating, and expressing. Sensory experiences should permeate the entire program to activate student involvement in experimentation and exploration. The nature of all of these experiences, their quality and adequacy, will strongly influence a child's image of himself, his establishment of values about learning and living, and consequently his development as an individual and a member of society.

Resources. A wide range of learning resources should be available to all students and staff. The variety, adequacy, accessibility, and appropriateness of such materials,

Is Your Middle School Relevant?

The accuracy of your answers to the following sample questions can help assure that the planning for your middle school will be as relevant as possible:

1. How do you plan organizationally to accommodate your instructional program to the learning needs and progress of your students?

2. In what specific ways will an individual student's schedule differ from that in the conventional junior high school?

3. What alternative approaches to instruction are to be provided?

4. What provision has been made for growth in independent study skills?

5. In what ways does the total school program coordinate the various subject fields? In what ways are the instructional endeavors in any one subject field linked to other areas of activity?

6. What is your plan for evaluating program effectiveness on a year-by-year basis? What base line data will you employ? How many aspects of growth will these survey? To what provisions for program modification for individuals and for groups will these studies and assessments lead?

7. What provision for building adaptations will be made for changes in program from year to year?

8. What factors in the *total* middle school program indicate that the emphasis is upon the child and his opportunities for success?

9. What provisions are being made to assure that the background, experience, training, and attitudes of the staff members are commensurate with child-centered rather than subject-centered approaches to working with middle school students?

10. What components of the middle school program will facilitate student and staff communication and enhance the scope and quality of interpersonal relationships?

How can factors that might inhibit communication and interpersonal relationships be eliminated?

11. What opportunities are afforded in the school program for orientation and exploration beyond the "academic" areas? What opportunities are afforded for familiarization with the worlds of work, living, and leisure? What provisions have been made for using the immediate and larger community as a learning laboratory?

12. How will the middle school program be articulated with the elementary and secondary programs? What provisions are included in the program for those students who have not yet mastered the basic skills at the elementary school level? What provisions are included for those students who are "ready" for facets of the curriculum that have traditionally been "reserved" for the high school?

13. How adequate are the facilities, staff, and program for the expansion of guidance and counseling during the middle school years?

14. How do you plan to identify and maintain an ongoing assessment of the aptitudes, interests, and capabilities of your students? How can you adapt this diagnosis and assessment to the teaching program?

15. What evidence have you that the purposes and functions of the middle school are understood and supported by the pupils, staff, parents, and community? What roles do students and parents play in the design, implementation, and evaluation of the middle school program?

16. What provision has been made for the selection and use of learning resources? Will the number, variety, and range of resources give students opportunities for appropriate experiences that will support the learning program and their special needs? What plans do you have to facilitate student and teacher access to these resources when they are needed?

equipment, and personnel should be commensurate with the program they are designed to support. A well developed and equipped educational center is the base for providing essential and effective student and staff resource services.

Organization. The pattern of organization of a middle school is not the only determinant factor in establishing a quality educational program designed to serve the needs of pre- and early-adolescents. A key lies in the program itself. However, once a program is developed, careful consideration should be given to selecting a flexible organizational pattern that will best accommodate it. Factors related to the organizational pattern of a school include time scheduling, grouping patterns, and personal assignments. An individualized and flexible program demands a flexible time schedule.

Grouping patterns appropriate to a flexible program might include heterogeneous, homogeneous, and multiage groupings, or varying combinations of these, as well as opportunities for independent work and study.

In determining personnel assignments, consideration should be given to the requirements of such approaches as team teaching, differentiated staffing, tutorial programs, independent study, or a combination of these, and how they may contribute to the needs of students.

Services. Essential to an effective school

Faculty work space for individual and group planning is essential.

program is a carefully developed plan which will ensure the necessary administrative and supportive services. These services include administration, guidance, health, special education, and maintenance.

Spaces. The basic consideration in designing the school plant is the accommodation of the facility to the program of the school. The middle school plant must reflect the transition from the concept of the self-contained classroom to the mobility of smaller groups and even individuals in later years. Variety, flexibility, and accessibility of spaces are prime considerations.

Provision must be made for a variety of spaces, ranging from large to small group areas, individual work spaces, staff resource centers for individual and group planning and for the preparation of a variety of teaching media, laboratories, and conference rooms. Flexibility of space can be achieved by means of mobile partitions, a variety of area dividers, and multipurpose facilities.

The facility to house a middle school program should be most carefully planned. It should represent the flexibility of the program, the rapidly changing child, the motivating atmosphere. Above all, it must in itself be a dynamic force, a live and living institution. ☐

An in-school television studio allows for the preparation of a variety of teaching materials.

The Middle School: What Is It?   •   25

EL 31 (3): 238-41; December 1973
© 1973 ASCD

DO YOU HAVE A

IN AN effort to provide general guidelines for use by educators in planning middle school programs, several tasks are necessary. First, the growing body of literature dealing with the middle school concept must be examined to identify important principles essential for these programs. Second, educational leaders prominent in developing and carrying on successful middle school programs must be interviewed for their views on what are important elements in a successful middle school program. Third, observations of actual middle school programs in operation will be necessary, as these will provide additional input for the development of needed guidelines.

Next, and certainly not the least important, is the consideration of the nature, the characteristics of the youth to be served, and the kind of society in which he lives. As in any worthwhile educational program, this is a most important consideration. The findings of such studies as have been made have led to the identification of 16 characteristics of the middle school and these are briefly cited here. These guidelines may be useful as criteria in evaluating existing or proposed programs, with a view toward determining whether they truly provide for students in the middle school years.

Criteria for Evaluating the Middle School

1. *Is Continuous Progress Provided For?*

Regardless of chronological age, students should be allowed to progress at their

These criteria can help you evaluate your program in terms of the characteristics of the pupils, the nature of knowledge, and the needs of the society.

own individual rates. This transescent stage of growth is one in which individual differences are most pronounced. Forcing students into a rigid chronological grouping pattern ignores this important developmental characteristic and defeats the effectiveness of educational plans. Instead, the curriculum must be built on continuous progress, permitting each student to move through sequential learning activities at his own rate.

2. *Is a Multi-Material Approach Used?*

While the basal text approach to teaching is the dominant approach today, it has disadvantages which give cause for serious concern. One of the major disadvantages is its inflexibility, since it assumes that all students respond to the same approach equally and progress through the text at the same rate. More consistent with the nature of the transescent is the use of a wide range of easily accessible instructional materials and a variety of activities to appeal to varied abilities and interests of students. The multi-material approach is consistent with the wide intellectual and physiological range of middle school age students who may compare with 7- to 19-year-olds.

3. *Are Class Schedules Flexible?*

In the traditional school, rigid time

MIDDLE SCHOOL?

NICHOLAS P. GEORGIADY*
LOUIS G. ROMANO

schedules often interfere with learning rather than serve it. Logically, the schedule should be based on instructional needs for various activities. To do this, the schedule should be varied and flexible, with changes made in class periods where these are necessary to fit the kinds of study activities being carried on.

4. *Are Appropriate Social Experiences Provided For?*

Some middle school age students are still children, immature, and not yet ready for more sophisticated social activities. Others are already adolescents with strong interests in social contacts with members of the other sex. Many are in transition between these two stages. Therefore, a program of social activities based on a high school model is inappropriate. Instead, there should be a program which provides for the unique needs of the transescent. These include wholesome social contact with members of the other sex through interaction in small groups, large-group activities in common areas of the school, club activities, dancing of the "mixer" type such as square dancing, and others. Serious dating and pairing off of couples are more appropriate at later ages.

5. *Is There an Appropriate Program of Physical Experiences and Intramural Activities?*

Highly competitive athletic programs are not appropriate for transescents, who are generally unprepared for the serious pressures these activities generate. Instead, physical education classes should center their

activity on helping students understand and use their bodies. A strong intramural program which encourages widespread participation is greatly preferred to a competitive, selective program of athletics which benefits only a few. The stress should be on the development of body management skills.

6. *Is Team Teaching Used?*

Every teacher possesses certain teaching strengths as well as weaknesses. In addition, transescent students benefit from a carefully planned schedule which puts them in contact with more than one teacher. However, they are not yet ready for the highly departmentalized approach of the high school. Therefore, a team teaching approach which utilizes teacher strengths in working with students individually and in groups is the logical way to meet the transescent's needs.

7. *Is Planned Gradualism Provided For?*

Another characteristic of the transescent is his eagerness to make more of the decisions concerning his own behavior, his own social life and choice of friends, his learning activities. While he is ready for some decision making at this stage, he is not quite ready for assuming the full burden of such planning, as the high school student must do. The transescent still requires some security and continues to depend heavily upon adult guidance. Therefore, the program of experi-

* *Nicholas P. Georgiady, Professor of Education, Miami University, Oxford, Ohio; and Louis G. Romano, Professor of Education, Michigan State University, East Lansing*

ences in the middle school should satisfy the transescent's needs for more independence while it also continues to offer him the assurance of sound adult guidance.

8. *Are Exploratory and Enrichment Studies Provided For?*

The transescent has a strong interest and curiosity in the world in which he lives. To provide for this, the middle school should offer a wide range of educational opportunities for the student. Electives should be part of the program of every student so that his unique needs can be met. Time should be spent in enriching the student's concept of himself and the world around him rather than confining him to learning only required subject matter in traditional form.

9. *Are There Adequate and Appropriate Guidance Services?*

The transescent has many problems troubling him and these often stem from the rapid physical changes he is experiencing. These problems require careful counseling from teachers and from trained guidance counselors. Group and individual counseling services are an important part of a successful middle school program.

10. *Is There Provision for Independent Study?*

Strong individual interests and curiosity characterize the transescent. This serves as a highly effective motivational force when there is adequate provision for independent study by the student, with the teacher available for assistance in planning and as a resource person. The value that this has in fostering self-direction by students makes it an important provision of the middle school.

11. *Is There Provision for Basic Skill Repair and Extension?*

Because of individual rates of growth, some youngsters have not entirely mastered the basic skills. These students require an extension of the program of basic skills development begun in the elementary school. There should be many opportunities to practice reading, listening, map and arithmetic skills, questioning, debate, etc. In some instances, the special services of remedial

teachers may be necessary for some students.

12. *Are There Activities for Creative Experiences?*

The creative talents of transescents require opportunities for expression. Students should be free to explore interests in many areas and to do so without pressures. Student newspapers, dramatic activities, art, musical programs, and others should be carried on in such a way that they encourage students to select, conceive, plan, and carry out activities in these areas.

13. *Is There Full Provision for Evaluation?*

The middle school program should provide a system of evaluation that is personal and positive in nature. If an individualized program is to be carried on, then the evaluation should be individualized. The student should be encouraged to assess his own progress and plan for future progress as well. The present common grading system using letters provides little information useful in understanding his progress and his areas of needed improvement. As part of an effective evaluation system, student-teacher conferences on a regularly scheduled basis are valuable. Additional conferences including parents can aid in reporting progress. The whole atmosphere in conducting evaluation should be constructive and positive rather than critical and punitive.

14. *Does the Program Emphasize Community Relations?*

The truly effective middle school is community-minded. It seeks to develop and maintain a varied program of community relations. Programs to inform, to entertain, to educate, and to understand the community are part of the basic operation of the school.

15. *Are There Adequate Provisions for Student Services?*

Providing adequately for the many needs of middle school students calls for a broad spectrum of specialized services. These should include health services, counseling services, testing services, and opportunities of both a curricular and a cocurricular nature. The important point is that the major needs of every student should be met by the school through its own services or through county or state services available to schools.

16. *Is There Sufficient Attention to Auxiliary Staffing?*

Every community has many human resources that can be useful in a school program. The middle school recognizes this and seeks to utilize people from the community in many ways. Volunteer parents, teacher aides, clerical aides, student volunteers, and others can do a great deal to facilitate the operation of the middle school program.

Many communities today are considering the development of middle school programs. Other communities have begun programs which they feel are middle school programs. Unfortunately, the pressures of time and an inadequate understanding of the true nature of a sound middle school program will result in disappointing or inappropriate programs in some of these communities.

The criteria outlined here can be useful in assuring effective planning for a new middle school program. They can also be useful in evaluating a middle school program already in operation. Use of these criteria in a carefully conducted planning or evaluation program can do much to facilitate the important decisions made by educators and citizens faced with the task of planning and implementing a middle school program which adequately meets the needs of its students. □

EL 23 (3): 217-23; December 1965
© 1965 ASCD

WILLIAM M. ALEXANDER
Professor of Education
University of Florida, Gainesville

EMMETT L. WILLIAMS
Associate Dean, College of Education
University of Florida, Gainesville

SCHOOLS FOR THE MIDDLE SCHOOL YEARS

WHAT school organization is best for pupils in that stage of development between childhood and adolescence? Some fifty years ago, the answer was to be a new *junior high* school for grades 7, 8 and 9. This pattern spread relatively rapidly, and a six-year (or six plus kindergarten) elementary followed by a three-year junior and three-year senior high has become the prevailing school organization in the United States.

Yet while these past decades of experience with this pattern have produced many significant and lasting features, there seems today increasing disenchantment with the schools for the middle school years. Some question whether the junior high school is a bridge between elementary and high school or a vestibule to the latter; others are urging change upon the typical graded, self-contained classroom of the elementary school, especially in its upper grades.

The 6-3-3 Plan?

Certainly there is not an adequate basis in research for strict adherence to the status quo. Research on school organization does not demonstrate the clear superiority of any one organizational arrangement over all others. Anderson's review (1) of research on organization in relation to staff utilization and deployment led him to conclude that ". . . recent research upon which policies of staff utilization and deployment must be based, at least temporarily, is woefully inadequate." What can be concluded from a review of the literature is that existing arrangements do not seem to satisfy some criteria for a school organization and a program consistent with psychological and physiological needs of pupils and relevant to modern societal demands.

For example, there is little research evidence to support, and some reason to question, the assumption that a junior high, separate and distinct from both elementary and senior high school, is a necessity because of the unique characteristics of the age group. On the contrary side, Margaret Mead (8) argues that the grades included in junior high "were postulated on age, and not on size, strength, or stage of puberty." As a result she observes that:

They have resulted inadvertently in classifying together boys and girls when they vary most, within each sex, and between the sexes, and are least suited to a segregated social existence. Also, they have divorced them from the reassurances of association with the children like their own recent past selves and older adolescents like whom they will some day become. When a type of school that was designed to cushion the shock of change in scholastic demands has become the focus of the social pressures which were once exerted in senior high school, problems have been multiplied.

From his viewpoint as a psychiatrist, Berman (2) sees the change from elementary to junior high school as quite poorly timed for children. He declares that "in the midst of deciding who they are, they shouldn't have to waste any energy finding out where they are." His opinion is that "during the highly volatile years of eleven through thirteen or fourteen, youngsters should have a familiar, secure background in which to operate."

Dacus' (3) study of pupils in grades five through ten raises interesting questions. On the criterion measures of social, emotional, and physical maturity, and opposite-sex choices, the *least* differences were found between pupils in grades six and seven, and pupils in grades nine and ten. Yet it is between these grades that our present 6-3-3 plan divides children.

The junior high school is most often defended on the grounds of the *bridge* function. It is supposed to serve as a bridge between the relatively untroubled, relaxed world of childhood and the more rigorous, stressful, disciplined world of high school. Johnson (6) declares: "In a world in which adults expound one set of values and espouse

another, in which schooling is prolonged, and economic dependence is protracted, and in which social life is largely outside the family, the value of a haven the junior high attempts to be is readily recognized" but notes that not all junior high schools have succeeded in this regard. He criticized the junior high for its tendency to imitate the senior high.

Hull (5) claims that junior high "is a poor investment," and that "it puts the unstable child at a most vulnerable period in his life in a situation more appropriate for older youth." On the other hand, it is commonly observed that today's children grow up faster in many ways. Havighurst (4) states that ". . . the adolescent today is more *precocious* and more *complex*. . . . He has many experiences *earlier* than his parents had these experiences." But does the present "bridge" school serve the intellectual needs of such children? Lounsbury and Marani (7) concluded from "shadow studies" in grade 8 classrooms across the country that the learning environment "was often unstimulating; there was lack of diversity in the program of required subjects; and there was little provision for individual differences among pupils."

Proposed: A Model Middle School

Along with the scholars and researchers cited, the present authors seriously question whether the currently dominant organizational arrangements for educating older children, preadolescents, and early adolescents provide optimum possibilities. New middle school organizations and programs (9) now being developed in various communities across the United States indicate considerable interest in experimentation with patterns differing from those now characteristic of the upper elementary and junior high school years. For consideration by others interested in developing alternative models, we offer the following as one set of possibilities for a model middle school.

Guidelines

A real middle school should be designed to serve the needs of older children, preadolescents, and early adolescents. Pupils would enter the middle school at the approximate age of ten years and would progress to the upper or high school at the approximate age of fourteen. Today's children in this age bracket need freedom of movement, opportunities for independence, a voice in the running of their own affairs, the intellectual stimulation of working with different groups and with different teacher specialists.

They are eager and ready for experiences quite different from those available in the typical elementary school. On the other hand, a congenial school environment for these children should be free of the rigidity of total departmentalization, the pressures of interschool competitions, and the tensions of older adolescent social functions that loom so large in typical junior high schools. The middle school would be planned to serve a truly transitional function from childhood to adolescence. Its organizational arrangements should foster growth from childhood dependence toward a high degree of self-sufficiency.

A middle school organization should make a reality of the long-held ideal of individualized instruction. Every pupil would be assigned a teacher-counselor who coordinates the learner's total program throughout the middle school years in conjunction with other teachers and specialists who know him. An adequate program of diagnostic services would permit teachers to plan individual deviations from standard programs.

Pupils would be scheduled to work in special instructional centers where they may either catch up on needed skills or branch out into further exploration. Programmed instructional materials and other individually paced approaches would be utilized, and self-directed learning emphasized. Nongraded arrangements could permit students to progress at different rates and to different depths.

A middle school program should give high priority to the intellectual components of the curriculum. There should be a planned sequence of concepts and skills for the general education areas of the curriculum. This does not imply emphasis on mastery of content of a narrow range of academic subjects, but rather that every effort would be made to create a climate in which learning is exciting and rewarding. What is required is not attainment of uniform standards but that every learner be challenged to perform well at whatever level he is capable of attaining.

In such an environment, intellectual pursuits would be as respected as the social and athletic components of the program, and children would be helped to see that learning can be its own reward uncluttered by any extrinsic sys-

The child of middle school age needs many opportunities to explore new interests. Special interest centers, competently supervised and operated on a flexible time basis, should provide individualized instruction in each curriculum area.

tem of grades as reward or punishment. Every pupil would be scheduled in a series of planned opportunities for developing both creative and disciplined thinking.

A middle school program should place primary emphasis on skills of continued learning. Direct instruction in use of various modes of inquiry and the discovery method helps children to experience joy in learning. In all studies, continued attention would be given to the learning process itself. Teachers would guide pupils in the use of sources, teach them to formulate questions, gather information and materials, and test hypotheses. Pupils would be given increasing opportunities to assume responsibility for portions of their own learning through use of independent study plans.

A middle school should provide a rich

program of exploratory experiences. The child of middle school age needs many opportunities to explore new interests. Special interest centers, competently supervised and operated on a flexible time basis, should provide individualized instruction in each curriculum area and also in such varied activities as reading, acting, photography, ceramics, typing, personal grooming, and many others. Boy Scout merit badge and Girl Scout proficiency badge work, and other youth programs could be incorporated into the school program under the coordination of the teacher-counselor. A portion of every pupil's schedule would include exploratory experiences.

A program of health and physical education should be designed especially for boys and girls of the middle school years. Direct instruction in essential knowledge of personal hygiene would be combined with regular participation in fitness activities, heterosexual group games, and carry-over sports activities. Adequate facilities and specialized supervision should be provided for a total range of physical and health needs including corrective and remedial programs.

An emphasis on values should underline all aspects of a middle school program. A middle school should offer unique advantages for helping children to formulate personal values and standards, and to analyze and question social attitudes and group behaviors. Children of this age are approaching or undergoing physical and psychological changes which they are striving to understand. They are beginning to establish new roles for themselves which sometimes conflict with adult expectations. They are increasingly aware of discrepancies between stated ideals and observed actions. Intellectually honest and emotionally calm exploration of these value areas with competent adult guidance would be a part of each pupil's regularly scheduled program.

The organization of a middle school would facilitate most effective use of the special competencies and interests of the teaching staff. Cooperative arrangements for teaching and guidance, special instructional center personnel, technicians and other aides, and ample supervisory staff would be utilized to enable each person to make his maximum contribution to the total program. Ample instructional planning time and in-service training opportunities would be provided for each teacher. The staff should be employed on a twelve-months contract with provisions for periodic study-leave.

The Curriculum Plan

The curriculm plan of a real middle school would consist of planned programs in three phases: Learning Skills; General Studies; and Personal Development. Every pupil would be scheduled into each of the three phases each year in school. The time requirements and the nature of the work in each phase would vary for individual pupil programs, but the general plan is seen as follows:

1. *Learning Skills Phase:* Continues and expands basic communicational and computational skills development begun at the primary school level, with increasing emphasis on use of library tools and skills of independent study. Skills for emphasis are identified and included along with content goals in each unit of work in all General Studies areas. A remedial program of skills development is conducted in special laboratory centers.

2. *General Studies Phase:* Includes those learning experiences which give the learner a heightened awareness of his cultural heritage and those other common learnings essential to civic and economic literacy. Content would be focused on major concepts and unifying themes drawn from the areas of literature, social studies, mathematics, science, and fine arts. Some of the instruction in this phase might be in groups of up to 100 pupils.

3. *Personal Development Phase:* Includes those experiences which fulfill personal and remedial needs, permit exploration of personal interests, and promote physical and social growth; health and physical education geared to the 10-14 year-old; individ-

The curriculum plan of a real middle school would consist of planned programs in three phases: Learning Skills; General Studies; and Personal Development.

ually planned experiences in foreign languages, typing, technical training, music, art, dramatics, journalism; student-managed enterprises; community work projects; advanced work in science, mathematics, and other areas of individual special competence and interest.

Organization for Instruction

The organization for instruction would be designed to facilitate an optimum curriculum and continuous progress for every pupil. Pupils in the middle school would not be expected to progress at the same rate or to the same depth. Neither would a student be expected to be at the same graded level in all of his studies. Planning and evaluation of an individual's progress through the curriculum should be a cooperative process based on diagnostic and evaluative data and involving his homeroom teacher, other teachers who work with him, and other special personnel, with the pupil himself involved at appropriate levels. Most children would remain in the middle school for a period of four years; however, some might be ready to move into the upper or high school after three years, and some might need to remain in the middle school for a fifth year.

The basic instructional unit of a middle school should be the individual. The significant organizational arrangements can be described by analyzing the various groups and centers through which an individual student would be scheduled.

1. *Homeroom Unit:* Each pupil would be a member of a homeroom group of about 25 pupils who are in the same year in school but are heterogeneously grouped on other criteria. A homeroom teacher-counselor, competent to give basic instruction in the General Studies area, and skilled in planning individual programs, would be assigned to each Homeroom Unit. The teacher-counselor would work out an individual program with each pupil, mandated by diagnostic and performance data and on the judgments of other teachers who also work with the pupil. The amount of time spent with the Homeroom Unit would vary with individuals, and typically decrease as a pupil moves from the first through later years in the school.

2. *Wing Unit:* A Wing Unit would combine four homeroom units and their teachers for cooperative planning and instruction in the General Studies area. The pupils in the Wing Unit would be in the same year in school but otherwise heterogeneously grouped. Four homeroom teachers, each representing a special competence in one of the General Studies areas of language arts, social studies, science, or mathematics would meet regularly to cooperatively plan the instruction for the 100 pupils in the Wing Unit. The teachers in the Wing Unit would function as a curriculum planning committee and as a teaching team. The team may arrange for some of the instruction to be in large groups containing all of the 100 students, and some of the work to be in small groups for interactive discussions, or instruction in basic skills.

3. *Vertical Unit:* The Vertical Unit, consisting of approximately 400 pupils and 16 teachers, would provide an evironment that is at once stimulating and secure, stable and flexible. The Vertical Unit (a "school within a school") gives the pupil a wider community in which to live, explore, and develop new social understandings. At the same time, this unit is small enough to promote a sense of identity and belongingness. All four year levels of the school would be represented in the Vertical Unit, and provisions for vertical acceleration through any area of the curriculum would

promote greater individualization and program flexibility. Younger students would have opportunities to work and plan with and learn from more mature ones, and the older student would have special opportunity to provide leadership within the Vertical Unit.

4. *Special Learning Centers:* The use of Special Learning Centers to serve the exploratory interests and the special and remedial needs of the middle school pupils would be a distinctive feature of the organization. Pupils would be scheduled for work in these centers on an individual basis for both short-term and long-term instruction in the Personal Development and Learning Skills portions of the curriculum. The centers should be adequately equipped and manned by special personnel competent to direct group study and individual projects. Special Learning Centers would include: library, reading laboratory, home arts, typing and writing laboratory, foreign language laboratory, arts and hobby center, music room, and physical education-recreation center. Centers would be operated on a flexible schedule and would be open to pupils after school and on Saturday.

The key to the implementation of a successful middle school program is a staff of adults of uncommon talents and abilities. The teachers must be as knowledgeable as possible in their chosen academic fields and must have training in the guidance and counseling of children of middle school age. A program of selection, recruitment, and training would be necessary to develop a staff with these special qualifications.

Obviously such a school would be expensive—perhaps costing up to half as much more per pupil than average

schools for children of the middle school years. But the loss of human potential in current educational organizations and programs for this age group may be far more costly.

If these ideas merit investigation, increased costs for their careful testing could surely be justified.

References

1. Robert H. Anderson. "Organizational Character of Education: Staff Utilization and Deployment." *Review of Educational Research* 34:455-69; October 1964.

2. Sidney Berman. "As a Psychiatrist Sees Pressures On Middle Class Teenagers." *NEA Journal* 54:17-24; February 1965.

3. Wilfred P. Dacus. "A Study of the Grade Organizational Structure of the Junior High School as Measured by Social Maturity, Emotional Maturity, Physical Maturity, and Opposite-Sex Choices." *Dissertation Abstracts* 24 (1963): 1461-62. University of Houston, 1963.

4. Robert J. Havighurst. "Lost Innocence—Modern Junior High Youth." *Bulletin of the National Association of Secondary-School Principals* 49:1-4; April 1965.

5. J. H. Hull. "The Junior High School Is a Poor Investment." *Nation's Schools* 65:78-81; April 1960.

6. Mauritz Johnson, Jr. "School in the Middle—Junior High: Education's Problem Child." *Saturday Review* 45:40-42, 56; July 21, 1962.

7. John Lounsbury and Jean Marani. *The Junior High School We Saw: One Day in the Eighth Grade.* Washington, D.C.: Association for Supervision and Curriculum Development, 1964.

8. Margaret Mead. "Early Adolescence in the United States." *Bulletin of the National Association of Secondary-School Principals* 49:5-10; April 1965.

9. Judith Murphy. *Middle Schools.* New York: Educational Facilities Laboratories. 1965.

EL 31 (3): 206-10; December 1973
© 1973 ASCD

Students, teachers, and parents work together to create, through time, a program that is integral to its middle-school clientele.

A Middle School: No Easy Way

NORMAN G. OLSON*

SCHOOLS for "middle-aged" children were new and few in Minnesota four years ago when Marshall Middle School began operation with 885 students. Fifth and sixth graders and their elementary teachers moved into two adjacent buildings occupied by seventh and eighth graders and their junior high teachers. We had a ready-made middle school on our hands and really did not know how to deal with it.

It was obvious that the traditional junior high school could not meet the needs of this age grouping. Therefore it was very necessary for the staff to do an assessment to determine the assets and liabilities of the situation. The results were:

Buildings: We had two adjacent, well-maintained buildings, one 1897 vintage and one 1935-style high school unit. There was plenty of space.

"Experts": Consultants who could answer all our questions were not available. We would need to be trailblazers.

Faculty: About 50 percent were trained and certified as elementary teachers and 50 percent as secondary teachers. There was

some apprehension about how well these teachers would work together.

We agreed that our primary goal must be to establish a learning climate that would allow every person in the school to develop a positive self-concept. This, we believed, is basic to living and learning.

Philosophy

After this goal had been established, we began to develop a philosophy so practical that it could be used daily as we struggled to put a program into action.

● *For the student:* Accept each student as unique.

1. Work toward individualizing instruction.

2. Encourage students to become more self-directed learners.

3. Develop instructional areas for large and small groups.

---

* *Norman G. Olson, Principal, Marshall Middle School, Marshall, Minnesota*

The Middle School: What Is It? ● 37

4. Arrange for adequate library and resource facilities for self-directed learning.

5. Consider the whole child by providing for his emotional and physical needs.

6. Abolish the traditional grading system. The learner becomes responsible for his own progress toward a goal which he has helped to set.

● *For the teacher:* Trust each other as professionals.

1. Provide the time and organization for teachers to work and plan together so that their talents might be used as fully as possible.

2. Encourage teachers to become planners and implementers rather than lecturers.

● *For the parent:* Foster closer cooperation between home and school.

1. Bring the child into the reporting procedure.

2. Provide a way for parents and teachers to communicate.

3. Keep the parents informed of goals, policy, and curriculum.

4. Encourage participation of parents through a parent council.

The Program

It is almost impossible to know hundreds of students well, yet each professional can know and keep track of 20 students. Therefore we initiated an advisor-advisee system which aided the individualized program that we had put into practice. Each faculty member was assigned 18 to 20 students (four or five from each grade level). These advisee groups stay together through four years of middle school as a relatively stable group with only four or five members gained or lost each year.

The chief task of the advisor is to build a positive, trusting relationship with each advisee. The advisor assumes responsibility for monitoring student progress, planning academic work with the student, encouraging participation in extracurricular activities, and being aware of developing interests, achievements, and problems.

The advisor also serves as the communication link between the school and the home. Formal advisor-advisee-parent conferences are scheduled every nine weeks. These are planned by the student and advisor using

Small group work enables a teacher to give middle school students the individual attention they require.

These years are a time for pupils to expand their interests in music and other arts.

materials gathered from teachers in all subject areas. The student invites his parents to school and explains his progress and projected plans in each subject area.

The emphasis is on success. Very often the student who struggles academically is pleased with his accomplishments in his projects and is proud to bring grandparents, brothers, sisters, and sometimes a neighborhood friend to the conference. This evolving relationship can foster an unbelievably strong cooperative spirit among students, faculty members, and parents.

The Mini-Schools

All students are involved in curricular offerings which include: language arts, social studies, science, mathematics, physical education, health and guidance, art, music, home economics, and industrial arts.

The staff is divided into academic multidiscipline teaching teams of four teachers who are basically responsible for the math,

language arts, science, and the social studies programs for their advisees. Consequently, all teachers on the team teach mutual advisees at all grade levels. Six of these multidiscipline teams function within the school. Two teams of teachers in special areas (music, art, home economics, shop, and physical education) are scheduled to serve mini-school teams.

Each teacher is also a member of a single discipline team. Some grouping to take advantage of a particular teacher's strength is arranged, but the basic goal of this team is to plan and devise curricular experiences within the subject area. For example, learning experiences planned by all social studies teachers are available to the multidiscipline teams. Much time and energy are devoted to organizing the basic content and skills within each curriculum with enough flexibility so that students can progress through content at various rates and depths using a variety of modes of learning. Alternative forms of learning experiences are essential in meeting the needs of all learners.

Process, Progress, and Problems

It was no small undertaking to meld a viable curriculum from the divergent teaching approaches of both elementary and secondary teachers. Implementing the philosophy, even though it is an uncomplicated statement, made unbelievable demands on staff time and student cooperation. The need for curriculum materials, most of which we had to put together ourselves, was an almost overwhelming problem. To compile these materials, single discipline teams were given common meeting time during the school day. It was necessary to cope with larger classes in order to accommodate these meetings. We were not without our critics during the three years this trade-off was in operation.

Single discipline teams of teachers were employed during the summer to put ideas that were found workable during the school year into final form. It took three school years of hard work and three summers of intense writing to gain enough expertise in various single discipline areas to be able to move productively to the multidiscipline teams. At that point the single-discipline curriculum became the tool that allowed the multidiscipline team to function. The school program began to achieve a good measure of its potential with the emerging maturity of the multidiscipline team.

The gathering and coordinating of teaching materials was another difficult challenge. We found much excellent material, but we were nearly swamped attempting to put it together in some form of continuous flow, to provide materials for alternate forms of learning, and to encourage continuous progress. To cope with this mass of work and materials, each major subject area developed a resource center staffed with a para-professional. No walls came down; we used spare classrooms, nooks, crannies, and hallways.

We continue to take first prize in the school district in the number of manila folders used and the volume of paper consumed.

A major strength in our school is a very professional faculty. Instead of being incompatible, the elementary and secondary teachers found their training backgrounds to be complementary. To keep the concern for the whole child of the elementary teacher and to add the in-depth subject matter expertise of the secondary teacher is a fine blend which has brought balance to our school philosophy and performance.

It takes communication, constant thoughtful in-service work, and continuous reflection upon the priorities set forth in the philosophy to keep this program operating smoothly. There is not much question that it would be easier and a lot less time-consuming to have a traditional junior high school or a traditional elementary school through the sixth or even through the eighth grade. However, we like what is happening to students and to faculty members in our school. Learning is exciting, fun, creative, and vital!

In conclusion, we see the advisor-advisee-parent relationship as the very heart

Emotional and physical needs play a large role in educating the whole child.

Comfortable couches, soft music, and volumes of paperbacks create a relaxed atmosphere for reading motivation and for teaching reading skills.

of the program. It represents a workable and necessary communication model. We have devised additional reinforcements to a workable communication network:

1. Student Council and its committees—meets weekly.

2. Student Advisor Council—meets weekly with administration. This group also helps to evaluate curriculum with single-discipline teams once each year.

3. Parent Council—meets monthly. One parent represents each homeroom on this council.

4. Faculty Council—meets each week. Representatives from the teaching teams research curriculum needs and reflect on the strengths and weaknesses of the school.

5. Single Discipline Teams—meet once a week. These teams make curriculum and scheduling decisions.

6. Multidiscipline Teams—meet once each week. This group "staffs" individual students, evaluates progress, and determines the learning experiences needed next by the 135 students of different ages in their charge.

Marshall Middle School is not a finished, finalized program, nor did we build it as a model. However, it is working for us, and we are well on the way toward achieving the goals that we have set.

We have worked hard and learned together as a staff and probably feel more professional now than ever before. Our school is becoming less "sit down and listen to me" and more "find out and do." Students like school and we believe we have fewer pupils who feel like academic discards.   ☐

PART 3

Middle Schoolers and Their Teachers

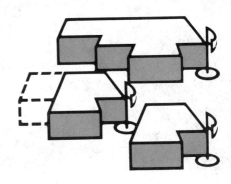

EL 31 (3): 228-29; December 19
© 1973 ASCD

THE

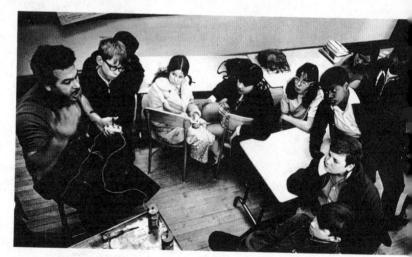

MIDDLE YEARS

MICHAEL J. SEXTON*

Middle school youngsters are eager, enthusiastic, inquisitive, often boisterous. They are also, at times, moody, awkward, and insecure. They are experiencing the contradictory pleasures and pains of a period of intense physical and intellectual development. No longer children, not yet adults, they are explorers in a challenging new world. Our task as educators must be to design a program to meet the special needs of this age group—and to nourish their budding enthusiasms.

Michael J. Sexton, Principal, Platteville Middle School, Platteville, Wisconsin. These pictures are taken from Dr. Sexton's all-photographic Ph.D. thesis, which is the subject of the book, Who Is the School? (Philadelphia: Westminster Press, 1973).

EL 27 (7): 686-91; April 1970
© 1970 ASCD

Teacher Attitudes: Subject Matter and Human Beings

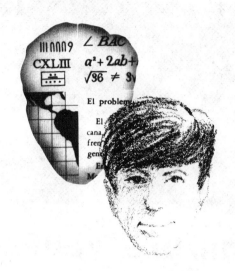

PHILIP J. HARVEY *

LORD ROCHESTER said, "When I was a young man, I had seven theories about bringing up children. Now I have seven children and no theories." The educator faces this situation head on, in the seeming impasse between subject-matter devotees and those who believe that the human child is more important than any body of subject matter.

This writer is increasingly concerned with the latter-day trend toward specialization in the secondary school, particularly in the junior high school. He sees beginning teachers emerging from their preservice preparation with up to 70 and 75 hours in their major areas, from a total of 125 to 130 hours. He watches the same neophytes go away to institutes and workshops, further to sharpen their knowledge and skills within their chosen specialty. He wonders about the wisdom of this much concentration on the subject matter to be taught, and the corresponding paucity of attention devoted to the human subject who is supposed to learn it. Then finally he concludes that much truth resides in one definition of an *expert* heard long ago: an expert is a man who knows more and more about less and less until finally he knows everything about nothing.

Truly we seem determined to shape our charges into the same narrow images of ourselves. Verily we drum facts, figures, and data ad infinitum into young heads, with little apparent regard for individuals and their inherent differences. Remmers and Radler, in their definition of the American teen-ager, described well his predicament:

A boy or girl whose energies are already sapped by the sheer prowess of physical growth, caught up in a whirl of school work and social activities in and out of school, confronted by decisions that will affect his entire life, confused by the shifting attitudes of parents, teachers, and society in general, all of whom doubt him and his behavior—and bewildered by the complex and rapidly changing civilization into which he must soon fit, assuming all the responsibilities of maturity.

Perhaps the indictment is too strong. Maybe the great majority of secondary school teachers have more concern for the individual pupil than has been credited. Reservations are certain to exist, though, when it is heard so often: "I have 150 different students every day, for 50 minutes each in groups of 30. I can't possibly get to know each of them as an individual. The best

* Philip J. Harvey, Principal, Walnut Junior High School, Grand Island, Nebraska

thing for me to do is teach to the big middle group"; or, "The ninth-grade English teachers will be very unhappy if we don't cover all the material." The list of examples could be extended indefinitely, by the reader or the writer.

It is readily recognized, and thankfully, that many junior high school teachers do care about their pupils as individuals. It appears, however, that a frightening number are too much subject-oriented, rather than primarily interested in their students.

Why this should be so presents a kind of paradox. The individual early adolescent is a tremendously complex entity, about whom we can know relatively little. Yet we can characterize him quite thoroughly, and without too much difficulty. By nature, he is inconsistent and unpredictable. He acts like an adult one day, a child the next. His is a time of change, especially physical and emotional. It is not his nature to sit quietly for a long period of time—for anything, let alone for a math, English, history, or science class. He may be a boy and a man, she a girl and a woman. He rebels. He wants discipline, and at the same time is struggling for freedom.

Care must be observed here. The early adolescent can be characterized, true, but those who work with him must look beyond the descriptive terms. You are an adult. You can't be like him and you can't think like him (though it helps to remember when!). Neither can he be like an adult. We tend naturally to impose adult standards on him. He tends naturally to resist. There is no such thing as the "average" adolescent, no such thing as "normal" behavior. There is "typically adolescent" behavior, but a tremendous variation is normal. It is the vitally important job of the teacher to distinguish the difference between misbehavior and what is normal for children at this age. Each is an individual.

Resistance to Authority

The period from 11 to 15 is an anti-teacher age. Teachers represent authority, and these youngsters are trying out their resistance to authority. In the elementary school, generally, respect and affection for the teacher are almost automatic. Junior high school teachers must earn respect and be worthy of affection. They are no longer *ex officio*. Incidentally, how many first graders do you know who dislike school? What is it that we do, or fail to do along the way, which creates such an aversion for school among so many young people?

More evidence exists, to indicate the proper perspective and approach to subject matter in the junior high school. Heffernan and Smith reported that the innate complexities of the early adolescent demand a program of education that is fully integrated and geared to the individual differences of the students. They cannot grasp the total venture if instructors make subject matter the nucleus of the entire program and ignore all the imperative needs of the individual at this most critical period. It is fallacious to assume that education can be "poured into" a child's mind, although there has been a great deal of "pitcher filling in junior high schools."

Subject matter, properly presented, with sincere and sympathetic understanding of adolescence, will focus all effort on goals and standards so intrinsic to his needs that each student will "soak up more basic skills and fundamental subject matter like a sponge." Emphasizing subject matter, increasing the work load with more and more rigid demands for homework assignments, and holding intractable attitudes toward the early adolescent and his needs will inevitably eclipse the basic intent of the junior high school program to be progressive and completely satisfying for every adolescent and teacher.

Further authoritative opinion was expressed by Bossing and Cramer, with regard to differing individual development and the importance of providing for it in the school program. They concluded that psychological development during early adolescence means a greater variance in available learning abilities than at younger or older ages. Some of these wide ranges in mental ability are due to rapid changes in physical, social, and psychological growth; irregular mental growth beyond 11 or 12 years of age; the fact that girls mature physically and socially one to two years ahead of boys; constitutional personality traits; and motivational influences from school, home, and community environments.

It is very important that administrators and teachers do not ignore or try to repress the late preadolescent's preparation and approach to early adolescence. The junior high school organization of classes, and especially in grade seven, should emulate that of the elementary school for at least a portion of the school day, but teacher-student planning and group classwork should be emphasized.

Fred T. Wilhelms recently presented a most interesting position. His argument was not really new, the proposition being that we could raise the educational dividends if we changed our educational investments.

The cogent, compelling reasoning behind his proposal merits serious consideration. He contends that a child's ability to do schoolwork can be raised by stimulation; sensory perception sharpening; verbalization; reasoning and logic; warmth, affection, and personal attention. While most such efforts to date have been concentrated on young children and the disadvantaged, Wilhelms suggests that the same tactics would apply to older students and to the "non-disadvantaged." He recommends that secondary schools should "invest boldly in teaching students to be able to learn better."

His summary bears repeating:

By long tradition, schools invest student time, teacher careers, and practically all their money in the business of putting across subject matter. Even when the resistance is stubborn, they fight it out on that line. If some ninth-graders read like third-graders, schools typically mount a massive remedial reading program (making some small gains, but generally winding up with low-mediocre readers after all). If students don't learn to write very well by producing "themes," English teachers press for lower student-faculty ratios so that they can have them write more of the same. Almost always, when there is trouble with subject matter, the instinct is to press harder on the subject matter.

It looks as if that's the wrong place to push.

With much less cost or effort we could turn children into the kind of learners for whom reading comes easily. Even a little time spent with an adolescent in enriching his concepts of himself and the life he wants to lead may make good writing part of his personal standard of living—and ease the burden on his composition teacher's weekends. It seems such nonsense to keep pushing harder and harder against the wall of reluctance and disaffection and sheer inability to handle the subject matter when we could do so much more by making our investments in the person.

Having studied the evidence, I am tantalized by the certainty that we could raise both cognitive and personal effectiveness. And, even though we still have a lot to learn, the technical difficulties don't look too bad. What we mostly need is the common sense to drop investments we know don't pay, and the nerve to try some more hopeful ones.

The tragic results abound, in our failure to see pupils as persons. It is apparent in the alarming rate of dropouts (or are they push-outs?). It is obvious in the long failure lists in most schools (have the pupils failed or have we?). It is conclusive in the high incidence of rejection in the armed services for physical, educational, and psychological reasons (who wants to be cannon fodder, anyway?). It is mirrored in the ever-rising rate of juvenile delinquency and adult crime. Most of all, it glares at us in the untold thousands who are left so far short of their potentials: unfulfilled, unhappy, and unable to make their optimum and badly-needed contribution.

Marilyn: A Case in Point

One such person was Marilyn. She was a pupil in a school where the writer taught. Her "case" is certainly not typical, but neither is it unique except in the particulars. She serves often as a personal reminder that people are indeed more important than things.

Marilyn was 14 years old, in the eighth grade, was five feet ten inches tall, and weighed about 120 pounds. An older sister, 17, was married during the school year, under unfortunate circumstances. Her father's paint store had failed that year, and he had been working at a succession of low-salaried jobs during the past several months. A new home under construction for the family burned under strange and suspicious circumstances.

Marilyn had never done very well in school, although she appeared to have "average" intelligence. During this eighth-grade year, her effort and attitude had gone downhill markedly. She was sullen most of the time, and refused to cooperate with her teachers or her classmates. Her classroom behavior ranged from silent non-participation to occasional outbursts of temper. As the year progressed, she became more and more a disrupting influence at school. She seemed to have few, if any, friends. She appeared to like boys, but was not popular with them.

Several weeks before the end of the school year, Marilyn and her parents were informed that she would probably have to repeat the eighth grade. The parents' attitude toward this was largely one of resignation, while Marilyn was strongly opposed to the idea. She was sure that she would do bet-

ter if permitted to go to the ninth grade. In the school system being discussed, the ninth grade was the first year of senior high school.

Shortly before the year closed, Marilyn's mother came to school, much concerned. She had found a note in Marilyn's room, which read substantially:

Dear Mom and Dad, The teachers still say that I'll have to take the eighth grade over again next year. I have been talking to Jesus about it. I told Jesus that if I am failed, I'll know that He wants me to join Him in Heaven. If they pass me, I'll know that He wants me to stay on earth. I love you very much.   s/Marilyn

How was this "case" handled, and what was the end result? The principal called together Marilyn's teachers. All of them were aware of her circumstances, and those of her family.

The principal made known to them the contents of her letter, and asked for their opinions and advice. "Just a bid for attention," said one. "She's going the same direction as her sister," offered another. "I can't

Middle Schoolers and Their Teachers   •   49

lower my standards to the point of passing her," remarked a third. Other and similar points were made. The principal tried in vain to get the teachers to consider other dimensions than subjects and grades.

At the end of the year, Marilyn received failing marks. She was retained in the eighth grade. She went home, took her father's shotgun, and literally blew off the top of her head.

A Teacher-Attitude Opinionnaire

Primarily for use among his own teachers, the writer has developed a teacher-attitude opinionnaire. It is crude and, to date, largely untried. In itself, it can do little, if anything, to change the attitude of a teacher. Neither would it be likely to do so, even if very highly refined.

Its purpose will be served if only its use can cause teachers to think more about their pupils first as individuals rather than as receivers/learners of factual subject matter. Hopefully it may act as the springboard to discussion and exchange of opinion.

For whatever it may be worth, it is included here.

Anyone writing with a bias, even prejudice toward a subject, can hardly expect to be regarded as objective. Many of the views presented here reflect such a slanted opinion, and without apology.

Some qualified authority has been offered, and much more exists. A good deal of personal opinion has been included. It is qualified by my 20 years of observation as a teacher and administrator in the public schools, 17 of them in the junior high school.

It is not suggested that we should return to the permissiveness of capital "P" Progressive Education. Neither is it advocated that we espouse anything like the deservedly ill-fated Life Adjustment Education of the late 1940's and early 1950's. Nor is it claimed that a lot of subject matter is not good or necessary.

Mine is, in fact, a rather simple plea. Since the pupil is an individual, let us approach his education with as much individuality as is possible. Let us help him to develop maximally as a complete human being. Let subject content take its proper place as a tool for use instead of as an end in itself.

The proverb is old, but true: "As the twig is bent, so the tree is inclined." Compartmentalize him strictly in the confines of subject matter rigidity, and the end product

Teacher-Attitude Opinionnaire	Agree	Disagree
1. The textbook is the curriculum.		
2. Attitudes are more important than facts.		
3. The teacher's primary obligation is to the individual pupil.		
4. Ability grouping is an undemocratic procedure.		
5. Rote memorization has little value.		
6. Mastery of subject matter should be a primary goal in the classroom.		
7. Textbook publishers should be more responsive to the wishes of teachers in the field.		
8. Knowledge unrelated to goals is indefensible.		
9. A nationwide standardized curriculum would be good.		
10. Understanding of different points of view is more important than universal agreement.		
11. Present teacher education programs encourage the inquiry or problem-solving approach to teaching and learning.		
12. Minimum essentials of subject matter mastery are needed.		
13. Teachers generally can do a better job when pupils are grouped by ability.		
14. Most secondary school teachers are more highly skilled in subject matter skills than in human growth/development.		
15. Each pupil as a person should be the paramount consideration of the teacher.		
16. Elementary school pupils generally like school better than their secondary school counterparts.		

will almost certainly be a narrowly-developed person.

And the choice is important, for as is indicated in *The Education of Henry Adams*, "A teacher affects eternity: He can never tell where his influence stops."

References

Nelson L. Bossing and Roscoe V. Cramer. *The Junior High School.* Boston: Houghton Mifflin Company, 1965.

James B. Conant. *Education in the Junior High School Years.* Princeton, New Jersey: Educational Testing Service, 1960.

Roland C. Faunce and Morrel J. Clute. *Teaching and Learning in the Junior High School.* San Francisco: Wadsworth Publishing Company, Inc., 1961.

Helen Heffernan and Maxine Smith. "The Young Adolescent." *California Journal of Elementary Education,* November 1959.

James L. Hymes. *A Child Development Point of View.* Englewood Cliffs, New Jersey: Prentice-Hall, Inc., 1955.

James L. Hymes. *Behavior and Misbehavior.* Englewood Cliffs, New Jersey: Prentice-Hall, Inc., 1955.

Eric W. Johnson. *How To Live Through Junior High School.* New York: J. B. Lippincott Company, 1959.

Gertrude M. Noar. *The Junior High School Today and Tomorrow.* New York: Prentice-Hall, Inc., 1961.

H. H. Remmers and D. H. Radler. *The American Teenager.* New York: Bobbs-Merrill Company, Inc., 1957.

F. C. Rosecrance and others. "Human Relations in the Classroom." *North Central Association Quarterly,* Winter 1963.

F. C. Rosecrance and others. "Human Relations in the Classroom." *North Central Association Quarterly,* Winter 1964.

F. C. Rosecrance and others. "Teacher Education for Human Relations in the Classroom." *North Central Association Quarterly,* Winter 1962.

Sister Marian Frances. "Discipline Is . . ." *NEA Journal,* September 1965.

Fred T. Wilhelms. *NASSP Spotlight.* Washington, D.C.: National Association of Secondary School Principals, May-June 1968. ☐

EL 31 (3): 214-16; December 1973
© 1973 ASCD

PERHAPS one of the most encouraging features of American education today is that we who advocate the middle school no longer feel we must devote an inordinate amount of time to justifying its existence. We have long urged the establishment of a segment of school organization which reflects the unique nature of youngsters who are in transition between childhood and adolescence. This kind of school now seems to have won acceptance.

Eichhorn (1966) has coined the term "transescence" to identify a transitional stage of development during which youngsters differ from younger children in the elementary school and from the high school's full-fledged adolescent. These youngsters are generally within the age range of 10 to 14. Growth of the middle school as a promising alternative to other organizational patterns for meeting needs of transescents has been phenomenal.

As a result of the wide acceptance of the middle school, attention has been diverted, to some extent, from the earlier controversy over which grades or ages should be housed in these schools. Interest now centers on what kinds of curricula are particularly suited to the needs and interests of transescents. Emphasis has been placed on a pluralistic curriculum, varying from one school district to another and from one school to the next within districts. This is fortunate inasmuch as facilities, materials, school populations, and teachers vary so greatly among schools.

Needed: Teacher Education for the Middle School

Most school administrators realize that, regardless of the motives of the school's establishment, the most modern facilities and materials and the best planned curriculum are of no avail unless the staff is prepared to work with transescents. Teachers make the difference in any school. The better prepared the staff is to work with youngsters of this age, the greater the likelihood that the middle school will be successful. Unfortunately, however, this is often not the case in

How Do You

The preparation program for middle school teachers needs four elements. A program at the University of Georgia seeks to exemplify these factors.

the traditional junior high school. Teachers selected for junior high school faculties have generally been prepared to teach in highly departmentalized senior high schools or as subject-matter generalists in the elementary school. Therefore, most junior high school staff members are recruited from the ranks of those prepared for a different level of education (Clarke, 1971; Brown and Howard, 1972).

If the middle school is to fulfill its function of providing a program suited specifically to the needs of the transescent, programs of teacher education must be developed that are aimed at the specific competencies needed by middle school teachers. Unless this is accomplished, the middle school may evolve into little more than a "junior-junior high school" or a "senior elementary school."

Characteristics a Teacher Needs for the Middle School

Perhaps it would help to look at a functioning middle school preparation program at the baccalaureate level. This writer has been actively involved in the development and implementation of the middle school

Prepare To Teach Transescents?

MARY F. COMPTON*

program at the University of Georgia. Following is a description of that program.

● *Early Opportunity To Make Realistic Professional Choices*

The teacher education program at all levels—elementary, middle school, and secondary—includes field experiences in the public schools on a regularly scheduled basis. These experiences are provided initially during the sophomore or junior years as a part of the orientation to teaching.

Through this early experience, prospective teachers can decide if they want to continue in the program designed for a specific educational level, transfer to another program, or pursue a career *other* than teaching. Students, therefore, are given the responsibility for making their own choices, and they are not locked into a program from which there is no retreat.

● *Content Field Preparation*

Once a student has elected to pursue a program leading to preparation for middle school teaching, he selects two fields of subject specialization. Alexander and his associates (1969) have stated that greater specialization is needed by middle school teachers than by those preparing for elementary teaching and on a different basis than that required of secondary specialists. Two fields of specialization are required in order to broaden the perspective of the teacher and

enable him to demonstrate the relationship between the various subject areas.

The program makes possible the combination of several subject fields, such as language arts and social studies, mathematics and science, art and music, physical education and science. Experiences in the teaching field component are selected by the student with the assistance of an advisor in each of his selected content areas. About 30 percent of the total program is devoted to this specialization.

● *General Education*

Approximately half of the middle school education program is comprised of general education. This component includes work in the humanities, social sciences, mathematics, science, and physical education. From within broad parameters determined by the university system, the student and his advisors may elect within each area specific courses which serve the student's needs.

General education in this program is viewed as a means of preparing the well-rounded individual whose profession is middle school teaching. It is recognized that preparation should be just as individually tailored for the prospective teacher as the program of the middle school is for the transescent it serves.

* *Mary F. Compton, Associate Professor of Education, University of Georgia, Athens*

● *Professional Preparation*

This preparatory program is based on the premise that prospective teachers need early and extended opportunities to work directly with transescents in the classroom. Thus, the program is field-based and will eventually be competency-based as the university moves toward a total competency-based teacher education program. Four professional phases are provided—a total of 40 weeks in middle schools.

During the first professional phase the focus is on the nature of the learner. Students are assigned to an interdisciplinary team and work for the most part in one of two areas of content specialization they have selected. Instruction is provided by university personnel in methods and materials with particular emphasis on this field of specialization.

The second phase concentrates on the child as a learner, with an emphasis on the helping relationship of the adult model. Experiences are provided here for the student to work in his second area of specialization with its methods and materials. Communications skills are also emphasized during this phase, particularly the teaching of reading.

The third phase is designed to integrate the two areas of specialization, to acquire competencies in the development and use of instructional media, and to develop skills in diagnostic teaching strategies.

Student teaching is the fourth and final phase, and this internship represents the capstone of the professional preparation program.

The phases of the professional sequence are planned as developmental. No student is permitted to enter the second phase, for example, until he has successfully completed the first. Each phase is staffed by an interdepartmental team of university specialists who not only are aware of the kinds of curricular and instructional strategies required in middle school but who, themselves, have been teachers of transescents. The university staff is responsible for supervising students in the portal middle schools, conducting seminars, advising students, and designing experiences which will meet student needs during each phase of the program.

The middle school program is individualized to the extent that no two student programs are identical. The 45 quarter hours devoted to the professional education component do not include specifically required courses. The middle school education team, therefore, has the freedom to design an individualized program for each student.

In summary, a flexible program of middle school teacher education has been instituted at the baccalaureate level at the University of Georgia. This program includes an opportunity for early professional choice based on experiences with transescents. This field-based program is individually tailored to meet the needs of the prospective teacher of these youngsters. This departure from a highly structured program of course requirements gives the prospective teacher a certain flexibility. Hopefully this flexibility will carry over into the planning of programs for transescents in which the teacher will later become involved.

The middle school teacher education staff at the University of Georgia does not feel that it has "arrived," nor has it "invented the wheel" in middle school teacher preparation.

There is still much work to be done. The staff does feel assured, however, that some important steps have been taken toward providing programs specifically designed for a unique group of professionals—the teachers of transescents.

References

William M. Alexander, Emmett L. Williams, Mary Compton, Vynce A. Hines, Dan Prescott, and Ronald Kealy. *The Emergent Middle School.* Second edition. New York: Holt, Rinehart and Winston, Inc., 1969.

Joan G. Brown and Alvin W. Howard. "Who Should Teach at Schools for the Middle Years?" *Clearing House* 46: 279-83; January 1972.

Sanford Clarke. "The Middle School: Specially Trained Teachers Are Vital to Its Success." *Clearing House* 46: 218-22; December 1971.

Donald H. Eichhorn. *The Middle School.* New York: Center for Applied Research in Education, 1966.   □

EL 27 (2): 191-93; November 1969
 INNOVATIONS IN EDUCATION

Developing Creative Abilities
in Adolescence

CHARLES E. SKIPPER
JACK A. DeVELBISS

THE rapid changes in our space age leave us bewildered and somewhat unsure about what tomorrow may bring. Yet we can be sure that in the future our society will place a higher premium on man's ability to develop and to use his creative talents.

Creativity has been defined by many writers, and most of their definitions include such terms as originality, curiosity, imagination, ability to sense problems, formulate hypotheses, and communicate the results. Creativity has also been defined as a successful step into the unknown, getting away from the main track, breaking out of the mold, being open to experience, and seeking new relationships.

Thoughtful educators today are following the lead of J. P. Guilford [1] and E. Paul Torrance [2] in experimenting with teaching procedures that hopefully will stimulate and develop the creative abilities found in all children.

The Living Arts Center in Dayton, Ohio, is designed to develop creative abilities in elementary and secondary school students by giving them, after the normal school day, opportunities for experiences in creative writing, dance, music, drama, and the visual arts. The Center, supported by Title III of the

[1] J. P. Guilford. "Creativity." *American Psychologist* 9: 444-54; 1950.

[2] E. Paul Torrance. *Guiding Creative Talent.* New York: Prentice-Hall, Inc., 1962.

Elementary and Secondary Education Act of 1965, uses such instructional methods as individual projects, small group discussions, and trips to cultural events.

Regular teachers are assisted by local artists who serve as part-time instructors. Students and faculty have been stimulated by face to face meetings with such guest artists as Lorin Hollander, John Ciardi, and Agnes Moorehead, who on occasion spend a week at the Center performing, lecturing, and demonstrating their special talents for the students at the Center, the regular schools, and the general public.

A Study of Creativeness

A two-year longitudinal study to determine the effectiveness of the program has just been completed. This study was conducted by selecting both an experimental and a control group from students in grades 7 through 10, on the basis of their performance on Torrance's "'Things Done on Your Own' Checklist," a 99-item index of creative abilities which asks children to indicate if they have written poems or stories, kept a daily record of the weather, made up new games, or the like. The groups were also matched for sex, grade in school, and school attended.

The results indicate that students participating in the program significantly increased their creative abilities when compared to the control group on selected dimensions of creativity.

Specifically, both male and female students in the program engaged in a greater number of cultural activities, both as spectators and as participants, than did the control group.

To determine the program's influence on thinking abilities, students were also tested on three aspects of creative thinking: ideational fluency, originality, and sensitivity to problems. Ideational fluency simply means the number of ideas that can be generated in a given amount of time, in response to a stimulus. On this test, the Categories Test by Cattell, students were asked to list things that are red or more often red than any other color.

Originality was determined by using Guilford's Plot Title Test, which requires the student to read a short story and then write as many appropriate titles as possible. Responses related to originality are clever comments which focus on the essence of the plot, comments that are uncommonly stated or stated with neat brevity, or responses that structure the information in the plot.

Sensitivity to problems was measured with the Apparatus Test by Guilford, which requires recognition of practical problems and suggested improvements such as structure revision, or use or operation of the structure.

Members of the experimental group significantly increased in their creative thinking skills when compared to members of the control group, with females gaining in ideational fluency, males gaining in sensitivity to problems, with no significant differences between experimental and control groups in originality.

Another dimension of creative abilities tested was esthetic sensitivity as measured by the Barron-Welch Art Scale. Barron's research has demonstrated that esthetic preference is related to rapid personal tempo, verbal fluency, impulsiveness and expansiveness, independence of judgment, originality, and breadth of interest. People scoring low tend to be rigid and to control their impulses by repression. Only the girls in the experimental group earned statistically higher scores on the Barron-Welch Scale when compared to the control group.

Self Perceptions

Probably the most important finding of this study is the differences in self perceptions between the experimental and control groups. Both male and female experimentals see themselves as more curious, having greater imagination, more resourceful, more expressive, more confident, more independent, and more ingenious than members of the control group.

The results of this investigation indicate that the Living Arts Center program has influenced its students to become more involved in cultural activities, increase the creative thinking abilities of ideational fluency and sensitivity to problems and esthetic preferences, and develop a sense of personal identity that is characteristic of creative individuals. The implication of this study for educators is that special programs that focus on developing the creative behavior of children can help them develop abilities and self understanding that in the past, with conventional programs, may have developed in a random way or may not have developed at all. Clearly the task for education today is to identify and nurture the human abilities that are required to paint a great picture, to compose a symphony, or to develop a space craft. The future of our society depends upon how well our educational system succeeeds in this effort.

—CHARLES E. SKIPPER, *Associate Dean of the Graduate School and Associate Professor of Educational Psychology, Miami University, Oxford, Ohio; and* JACK A. DEVELBISS, *Division Chairman, Fine and Performing Arts, Sinclair Community College, Dayton, Ohio.*

EL 31 (3): 211-13; December 1973

Must Middle Grades Education Consist of "Cast-Offs"?

CONRAD F. TOEPFER, JR.*

Pioneering efforts by Educational Leadership Institute and ASCD's Working Group on the Emerging Adolescent Learner have created six new information packages. These present curriculum improvement and teacher skill development for the emerging adolescent years.

THE work of the ASCD Working Group on the Emerging Adolescent Learner was keenly attuned to the dilemma of "Secondhand Rose" as depicted in the song made popular at that time by Barbra Streisand. The members of the working group concurred that in virtually all aspects of his school experience the emerging adolescent has been subjected to a wide range of "hand-me-downs." Whether it be school plant facilities, scheduling conflicts, teacher certification and preparation, or instructional materials, the middle school is like the middle child in many families, who receives the outgrown or cast-off clothes of his or her elder siblings!

Theorists continue to define the growing body of data and evidence supporting the unique nature of the emerging adolescent as a learner and personality. Nevertheless, few school districts have considered such needs in developing programs and educational opportunities designed to meet these validated imperatives. New high schools are built and junior high and middle schools try to make do with old, former high school plants. Scheduling and bus transportation prerogatives focus upon either high school or elementary school concerns, and instructional materials budget cuts seem invariably to put their paring knife to the middle unit of the school system first.

"Retreads" Make Poor Teachers

Most critical over the years has been the "retread" approach to staffing schools for emerging adolescents. Until the appearance of the recent "lighthouse" efforts in Florida and Georgia, preservice teacher education programs for teachers in the middle grades have almost totally obviated any preparation to cope with the unique problems of emerging adolescent learners or to provide teachers with a specific attitude and expertise toward

* *Conrad F. Toepfer, Jr., Associate Professor, Department of Curriculum Development and Instructional Media, State University of New York, Buffalo; and President, New York State ASCD*

clarifying developmental emerging adolescent needs. With a major national effort to specify preservice teacher education for the middle grades apparently still far off, the critical level for refinement viewed by the ASCD working group was and continues to be the in-service avenue. The relatively minor focus of most graduate school programs upon concerns of middle grades teachers led to the decision to develop some specific means for discrete, tactical support of teachers and administrators in middle grades looking to refine their programs. To this end, it was decided that "written materials only" would not provide such a means beyond the existing literature. The members of the working group decided that a "hands-on" approach which could be utilized at the local school level was something which a total information package could best provide. For a description of the development of the project, see: *ASCD News Exchange* 13 (5): 3-5; September 1971.

ELI-ASCD Packages Give Hope

Out of these efforts have come six information packages including filmstrips, audio cassettes, records, library and reference cards, and position papers designed for use in local in-service programs concerned with the improvement of middle grades instruction for emerging adolescents. The six packages are in the areas of: Educating Emerging Adolescents—Some Operational Problems; Implications of the Curriculum—Boyce Medical Study; The Nature of the Emerging Adolescent; Learning Strategies for the Emerging Adolescent; The Impact of Social Forces on Children; and Adult Models for the Emerging Adolescent. Each of these areas was viewed by the working group as critical to the refinement of curricula and the development of teacher perception of the nature and educational needs of the emerging adolescent learner. Thus the expectation for the utilization of the information packages is both for curriculum improvement as well as teacher skill development in a more realistic understanding of the emerging adolescent.

In addition to the field testing of the

packages in their developmental stages under ASCD auspices, follow-up utilization causes optimism in projecting the usefulness of the packages in local school districts. During the past year the packages were used in a series of continuing in-service activities with middle school teachers in the Scranton, Pennsylvania, School District, with encouraging results. Personnel from a number of school districts also utilized the packages in an in-service institute held in the summer of 1973 at North Adams State College in Massachusetts, with similar enthusiasm from participants.

The intent here is not to imply that when mixed with water the six information packages will result in instant refinement of emerging adolescent school programs. It does appear, however, that they represent a specific source of information and help for schools seeking to improve educational experiences in the middle grades. Perhaps some of the success in their utilization comes from the fact that they were prepared specifically for use in the middle grades and not "watered down" from an existing high school level series. These materials were developed by educators with a specific concern for the needs of emerging adolescents rather than for forms of schooling or grade level demarcations. It is felt that both of these concerns are pivotal to continuing efforts to improve education for emerging adolescents in the middle grades.

There is certainly room and need for the development of additional materials for use in developing local programs and improved educational experiences for emerging adolescents. However, these packages as developed by the ASCD Working Group on the Emerging Adolescent Learner do appear to be an important source of help to local school districts interested in improving their instructional program in the middle grades. They also point clearly to the importance of ASCD's taking on a continuing commitment to work for the improvement and humanization of the educative experience for the learner housed in the middle of our system of schooling. It is only as we recognize his uniqueness as a learner and human being that we

Photo by Michael J. Sexton

Learning materials must be specifically designed for the unique instructional needs of the emerging adolescent.

begin to identify how education must be reorganized if it is successfully to utilize the emerging adolescent's capabilities for positive growth. Our failure to do so will force him or her to continue to cope with the dispensing of information on the basis of administrative convenience rather than working within his or her capacities at this developmental stage.

The six information packages developed by the ASCD Working Group on the Emerging Adolescent Learner represent a definitive but beginning step in developing means to revitalize education for emerging adolescents in terms of their capabilities as learners in a critical stage of human development. They represent a "firsthand rose" rather than another "hand-me-down" set of pants with the cuffs altered. Obviously, more than these beginning efforts will be necessary if we are to get beyond the "retread" approach in developing education at this level. We hope, however, that educators throughout the country will examine these materials carefully and utilize them to initiate local efforts to improve their educational offerings in the middle grades. □

EL 23 (3): 200-204; December 1965
© 1965 ASCD

THE ADOLESCENT INTELLECT

MAURITZ JOHNSON, JR.
Professor of Curriculum and Instruction
State University of New York at Albany

AMERICAN adolescents have been exceedingly well studied. They are known to be bothered by acne, to reject adult authority, and to have an awakening interest in the opposite sex. They conform slavishly to peer group standards, and, except for a few abnormal ones, they are either overly aggressive, submissive, withdrawn, or characterized by psychosomatic symptoms. All but about 95 percent are juvenile delinquents. The female type reaches puberty approximately two years before her male age-mates and between ages 11 and 13 exceeds them in height as well as in school marks.

According to James Coleman, adolescents value popularity and athletic prowess; according to Robert Havighurst, they have nine developmental tasks to carry out; according to Erik Erikson, they have four such tasks, the first being to achieve industry while working toward identity, fidelity, and intimacy. It is widely recognized that they have changing bodies, ambivalent feelings, and numerous problems, worries and needs, but until recently few have suspected that they also have intellects.

Indeed, the very term "intellect" is rare in the literature of education. The crucial concept has been "intelligence," a global capacity for solving problems, according to David Wechsler; existing in three forms—theoretical, social and mechanical—according to E. L. Thorndike; composed of general and specific factors, according to Charles Spearman; and increasingly differentiated at puberty into some seven or more primary mental abilities, according to L. L. Thurstone. But intelligence has been viewed as an attribute that is largely determined genetically, subject to cumulatively substantial, but nevertheless comparatively limited, modification by environmental influences. Educators have seen intelligence essentially as the raw material for their work, providing possibilities and imposing limits. Their preeminent goal has been "intelligent behavior," overt and observable, rather than the development of any such inferred abstract quality as intelligence, much less one as abstruse as an intellect.

Finally, however, a time was reached when the world had been so drastically changed by intellectual efforts that attention was drawn to the intellect's increasing importance. Belatedly, scholars began to participate in curriculum reform.

Curriculum Reform

Jerome Bruner called attention to the value of students' discovering fundamental relationships among key concepts within a disciplinary structure and suggested that intellectually honest discovery in some form is possible with children at any age. Joseph Schwab stressed the importance of both the conceptual and the syntactic structures of disciplines. Philip Phenix defined learning not as a change in behavior but as the discovery of meaning, and he classified meanings as symbolic, empiric, aesthetic, ethical, synoetic, and synoptic. B. O. Smith took a new look at the teaching act and saw logical operations on subject matter as an important element. We were reminded of Jean Piaget's earlier contention that in acquiring meanings children pass through a stage of concrete operations before entering, sometime before reaching puberty, the stage of formal operations.

Piaget's studies show that, while the sequence in which stages are reached is invariant, the specific age is affected genetically, experientially, and culturally. Even in Martinique, where development is slower, the stage of formal operations is reached before the period known in America as the junior-high-school years. Moreover, it has been demonstrated that when children are given appropriate intellectual experiences, prevalent notions about readiness prove to be untenable. Robert Davis has found that fifth graders can not only readily discover truth sets for open mathematical statements, an achievement traditionally considered difficult for ninth graders, but can also invent mathematical laws of their own, something that students are seldom encouraged to do at any level. Patrick Suppes has successfully taught young children to engage in mathematical reasoning.

Professional reaction to these demonstrations and to the shift in goals and changes in curriculum that they imply has been interesting and, to a degree, disturbing. In many schools, to be sure, enlightened teachers and administrators have eagerly seized the opportunity to experiment with radically revised curriculum arrangements and new instructional approaches that challenge students and inject an unwonted intellectual vigor into their schooling. But from those who have resisted have come expressions of concern regarding undesirable "pressures" on children and youth and protestations that social-emotional development is fully as important as intellectual growth, that education should provide practical preparation for living and earning, that learning experiences should be "life-like," and that recent reforms represent a return to "subject-matter centeredness."

These are sincere reactions and understandable ones, given the clearly demonstrated and freely admitted lack of intellectual interest in the society as a whole and among a large segment of the teaching corps. Of all the reactions, however, the most disturbing is that based on the erroneous belief that the current ferment is a retrogression to the uninspiring peddling of vast quantities of unrelated, out-dated, inert factual minutiae for rote memorization by apathetic students. Many lackluster traditional teachers who characteristically practice such vapid peddling share this belief and mistakenly applaud recent developments on the assumption that their practices are vindicated thereby.

Given this misconstrual of intellectual activity on the part of some and the antipathy toward it on the part of others, it is extremely difficult to assess the true characteristics of the adolescent intellect. Certainly it is no compliment to junior high school students to assert that most of them are quite as capable of engaging in intellectual activity as is the average adult.

Those who come from homes in which intellectual interest exists, located in communities in which intellectual achievement is valued, and attending schools in which intellectual activity is stressed at all levels—those adolescents can be expected to conceptualize, reason, and engage in inquiry of a far different order from that which can be expected where one or more of these three factors is missing. Significantly, the only place where the vicious cycle can be broken is in the school, though perhaps this is impossible without a substantial infusion of new teachers who themselves have a strong intellectual orientation and commitment.

A Sound Base

Unfortunately, beginning teachers of such persuasion will not long remain in a school where the principal's primary concern is the athletic program and where only a few teachers read, have a scholarly interest in their subjects, and prefer serious discussion to faculty lounge gossip. Where enough kindred spirits are to be found, however, a substantial transformation of the junior high school, giving greater play to the adolescent intellect, can be effected.

Underlying any such transformation is a basic change in the "climate" of the school. Some junior high schools today are characterized by a repressive rigidity and stultifying stagnation; others by a sentimental indulgence of the frivolous and the trivial. Neither type exalts either ideas or inquiry. The desired atmosphere is one in which the examples set by teachers and the policies set by the school give clear indication that intellectual pursuits are valued above all others. In view of the long-standing entrenchment of countervalues, the mere honoring of intellectual accomplishment will probably be insufficient. Temporarily, at least, it may well be necessary not only to ignore and de-emphasize, but actually to discourage, occasions for extolling popularity and athletic performance.

Equally as important for adolescent intellectual development as a hospitable atmosphere in the junior high school is an appropriate grounding in the elementary school. A sound conceptual base must be established through long experience with concrete operations in the empirical realm. Even more vital, however, is close attention to linguistic and mathematical symbolic structures. The outlook in mathematics is hopeful, with the increasing emphasis on correct terminology, properties of the real number system, and unifying mathematical principles. In the area of reading, however, nothing short of a complete overhaul of the system that prevails today seems likely to bring about the necessary reform.

Regardless of how unsatisfactory for currently accepted purposes the insipid stories in conventional readers and the excessive reliance on a look-say approach may be, these defects are minor compared to the general overemphasis on entertainment and neglect of language structure. Children must at an early age come to view reading primarily as a source of ideas and information and secondarily as a means of recreation. At the same time, whether pupils are encouraged to recognize words at sight or decode them analytically, they must attend not merely to the meanings of words but to their functions and positions in sentences.

Intellectual Emphasis

By the time they reach the junior high school the majority of students should be ready for formal operations. They should then regularly engage in framing definitions, indentifying assumptions, dealing with cause-and-effect relations, classifying individual phenomena, generalizing from recurring particulars, and determining necessary and sufficient conditions for a conclusion. In short, they should, in the terms of Robert Ennis's definition of critical thinking, become able to assess statements correctly. Concurrently, they should be gaining fundamental insights into matter, energy, and biological phenomena and acquiring a conceptual basis for explaining man's interaction with his geographical environment and with his fellow men, through economic, political and social institutions. Students should continue to advance in mathematical sophistication instead of endlessly applying elementary concepts to every conceivable practical situation.

These intellectual activities assume their rationale under a conception of general education which, in the terminology of Harry Broudy, B. O. Smith and Joe Burnett, emphasizes the "interpretive" use of knowledge. A junior high school guided by this conception will abandon the notion of prevocational exploration and premature vocational decisions. It will consider its intellectual emphasis the most practical kind of preparation for both the vocational and the leisure-time realities of the future, and its teachers will refuse to acknowledge students' demands to know the specific practical value of their studies. It will protect students from having to attempt to devise solutions to complex social problems until they have mastered the fundamental concepts of the relevant disciplines and are aware of both the assumptions and the methods of inquiry underlying the disciplined search for truth.

Particularly bothersome is the problem of providing a coherent program in the humanities. Efforts must be made to maintain the highest possible artistic standards in selecting works for study in literature and the fine arts. The cultivation of critical tastes demands a radical departure from current desultory efforts in the arts and requires continuation throughout the senior-high-school years, which is impossible until the diverse elective program at that level is abandoned.

It is an affront to adolescents to assume that they cannot or will not respond to a program with a serious intellectual emphasis. Provided with a suitable background and placed in a setting in which intellectual activity is not deprecated, most of them are quite capable of dealing formally with abstract notions that serve to explain the world around them and invest their experiences with meaning. Dealing with ideas diverts adolescents from their preoccupation with themselves. Even the slower learners can more readily grasp significant ideas than retain masses of inconsequential facts. By definition they cannot progress as rapidly as the average adolescent can toward the consideration of more complex concepts, and the program must account for such differences. A curriculum that is arranged on the basis of the level of intellectual comprehension required cannot, of course, be bound to conventional grade designations. Until a more coherent curriculum has been arrived at, however, teachers will have to rely on the use of a discovery approach to gauge the intellectual level at which a particular group of students is ready to function.

Charles Armstrong and the late Ethel Cornell found that most individuals pass through two cycles of mental growth, the second beginning around puberty, often after a plateau period of relatively little progress. Possibly this plateau is the result of the school's failure to confront the young adolescent with a timely challenge to his changing intellect. It seems unlikely that the physiological and emotional aspects of maturing at that stage usurp so great a proportion of some fixed reserve of psychic energy that little is left for intellectual activity. Indeed, when an individual is putting away childish things, he is anxious to think about serious matters.

The adolescent intellect deserves more respect and greater expectations.

EL 23 (4): 290-92; January 1966

THE ADOLESCENT
AND HIS TIME

WANDA B. MITCHELL
Former Chairman, Speech Arts Department
Evanston Township High School, Evanston, Illinois

THIS is an age of computer registration numbers, area code telephone numbers, and dial-a-tape French lessons. Small wonder that a youth described one phase of his new life in an Army barracks as "wall-to-wall brothers." Students are herded into massive lecture halls and catalogued according to the "normal distribution" curve.

Today's educational programs sometimes make it easier for a student to master calculus in high school than to discover himself and maintain his individual identity. What chance is there for dreams, for identifying one's self, for thinking through the purpose of one's life, for introspection? Most capable students would find it easier to answer a question on intercontinental missiles than the one presented to *The Man in the Gray Flannel Suit*: "What is the most important thing about *me?*"

This discovery of self is one of the essentials of total education. Henry Ward Beecher described education as "the knowledge of how to use the whole of one's self. Many men use one or two faculties out of the score with which they are endowed. A man is educated who knows how to make a tool of every faculty— how to open it, how to keep it sharp, and how to apply it to all practical purposes." A curriculum which makes no provision for the discovery of self is inadequate in preparing youth for meaningful existence.

How can the curriculum provide opportunities for self-discovery? One way is suggested by UN Ambassador Arthur Goldberg in a *New York Times* article while he was Secretary of Labor:

In a complex, modern society like our own, art of all kinds is called to one of the essential services of freedom—to free man from the mass. Art, whether on the stage, in a gallery, or in a concert hall—asserts the supremacy of the individual. The insight of the artist leads to cultural discovery for all of the people.

It is no happenstance that the government is now supporting creative and performing arts centers throughout the country. Such activities are following the recommendations of the White House Conference on Children and Youth that "more emphasis be placed on cultural activities to provide children with creative outlets and increase their appreciation of beauty and their interest in the arts." Such activities provide for individual expression for "the world of the artist is supremely the world of the individual."

Arts and the Self

Sydney Harris, Chicago *Daily News* columnist, writes:

What is immensely appealing, in a deep human sense, about the arts is that they remain one of the few areas in which true individualism can flourish; in which the creator and performer is a person directly communicating with other persons; in which his ancestors, language, connections, and superficial traits are totally subordinated to his professional skill.

Mr. Harris warns us of the dangers to society when this "creative urge goes sour," when a youngster's creative energy is not channeled in satisfying and productive ways.

It is often the brightest and most potentially talented slum youngsters who become the leaders in gang violence; they are the little Napoleons who do not know what to do with their gifts except devise ways to retaliate against the social order. Some of them, of course, are psychopathic personalities; but many are what Lindner rightly calls "rebels without a cause."

A realistic curriculum provides such rebels with a cause through activities such as art, music and drama. Rita Criste, director of the Children's Theater of Evanston (Illinois) describes the magic experience of seeing James Barrie's *Peter Pan* as

... all alive with sound and color and movement. [It] gives each child an impression of beauty and wonder which will last not for one day but for a lifetime. . . . By repetition of certain themes through the theater we work toward understanding, compassion and responsibility. To what end do we develop matters technologically without a balance of maturity in matters moral and ethical?

Such creative experiences are equally necessary for the total development of the teen-ager described by Mardell Ogilvie in *Teaching Speech in the High School*:

High school students are complex individuals—awkward, emotionally unstable, anxious for approval of their peers, longing for independence from their families, and wanting solutions to moral, philosophical, and religious problems. Much of the time they secretly play roles. They walk, talk, dress, and act like those they idolize. They identify themselves both with real people, and with people in books. Because of their complexity and their desire to play roles, creative drama serves a real need for them.

Relating to Others

Thus, the curriculum needs to provide each student with opportunities for identifying, developing and expressing his individual personality. A corollary is the need to help that individual develop satisfying relationships with others. There are certain personal skills and human relationships necessary for successful living in a democracy that cannot be learned by writing essays, that cannot be mastered by memorization, that cannot be acquired in a science laboratory.

Young people learn to be kind only by working with other people; they learn to be tolerant only in human relationships; they learn to influence the conduct of others in a laboratory of work with other human beings whose rights are equal to, but not necessarily the same as theirs. Every personal contact within the school is part of this process. Activities such as student government, the school newspaper, traffic patrol, class parties, the senior prom, the May Day queen, the talent show, the old clothes collection are therefore an important part of the school program—not to keep students off the street, not to keep them wholesomely occupied, not to prevent them from becoming juvenile delinquents, but to equip them with skills necessary for the functioning of the democratic process.

A curriculum which provides for self-identification and satisfying relationships with others is not totally fulfilling its purpose if it makes no provision to assist the student in mastering the world of work and leisure. A realistic curriculum has the responsibility of developing not only skills and craftmanship, but *also attitudes* toward work.

Are businessmen and industrialists justified in their criticism of the products of the public schools? In a recent article in the Chicago *Daily News*, the president of one of the nation's largest advertising agencies said:

The U.S. is going through the great era of the goof-off; the age of the half-done job. The land from coast to coast has been enjoying a stampede away from responsibility. It is populated with laundrymen who won't iron shirts, with waiters who won't serve, with carpenters who will come around some day maybe, with executives whose minds are on the golf course, with teachers who demand a single salary schedule so that achievement cannot be rewarded . . . with students who take cinch courses.

The mediocrity of salesmen is only a part of our national pattern of always being willing to settle for something less than the best.

No curriculum can progress fast enough to train students for jobs which come into existence with each technological advance, but it can and must guide them in the development of attitudes toward work and toward the increasing hours of leisure time. How adequately do the music program, the physical education department, the drama program, the book reports in English, the geography class, the modern language course prepare the student to spend his long vacations in profitable creativity, travel, reading, and refreshing physical activity?

Anyone associated with modern adolescents is aware of the pressures with which they are faced. The academic push begins early, as was depicted in a recent cartoon showing a preschool youngster whispering into Santa's ear: "Please, can you get me into Harvard?" The increasing number of emotional problems related to these and other pressures serves as a constant reminder of the need to develop a curriculum which will include opportunity for self discovery, activities for achieving satisfying human relationships, and the development of skills and attitudes for work and play.

EL 23 (3): 190-93; December 1965
© 1965 ASCD

Today's Junior High Students

WILLIAM W. WATTENBERG
Program Coordinator, Educational Psychology
Wayne State University, Detroit, Michigan

IT IS always hazardous to compare any age group with its counterpart in times past. In every generation, adults see in young adolescents a frightening assortment of contrasts with "the way kids were when we were their age." It is all too easy to react emotionally to newspaper headlines or to the noisy jostling at the school entrance.

If we attempt to resist stereotyped thinking and to be objective, there seem to be three major ways in which today's younger adolescents differ from those of previous generations:

1. Thanks to better nutrition, they do mature somewhat earlier.

2. Thanks to better education, they know more and have greater intellectual sophistication.

3. No thanks to a combination of causal factors, they are more dichotomized than any previous generation. It is this difference, its causes, and possible educational implications which will be the topic of this article.

In almost every generation of which we have knowledge there has been a tendency for young adolescents to adopt fads which set them apart from "little kids" on the one hand and adults on the other. Although not all were affected with equal intensity by the fads, and although the fads could be in many areas— language usage, clothing, dance patterns, and social customs—nevertheless at any one time in any one area there was likely to be a single fad.

The In's—The Out's

What has happened that is relatively new is that today there tend to be *two* fads, each picked up by a different group. In many American schools, we have on the one hand a group of youngsters who are "in." They tend to follow somewhat sophisticated clothing styles. The terms by which they are identified vary from community to community and from year to year. Typical are "varsity," "Sosh," "Frats," "Ivy," and "Tweeds."

The contrasting group of youngsters, for whom the very names are indicative, may be known as "grease," "hoods," "trolls," etc., and are likely to consist of visibly alienated youth. The boys are likely to combine a markedly feminine appearance with clothes that make them look like tough characters. The girls may adopt outlandish hairdos and extreme clothing styles.

This dichotomizing of the youth population is by no means solely an American phenomenon. Its appearance in England, for example, led to combat between the "Mods" and the "Rockers."

What is of fundamental concern is that this dichotomy seems to be but a surface manifestation of the fact that the disparities among our youth are increasing. It is possible that as programs launched under the Economic Opportunity Act of 1964 and the Elementary and Secondary Education Act of 1965 take hold, these disparities may be reduced. Nevertheless, at the present moment these divergencies are so much a fact that we must seek for causes and solutions.

One factor probably has to do with the size of our educational units. Although big schools make for some advantages in specialized offerings and specialist teachers, they also can lead to impersonal handling. In small units, every boy or girl has a role, an active role. As shown in the Barker and Gump studies, *Big School; Small School*, in large units many pupils have to be a passive audience for the active "in's." It is not surprising, then, that as a general rule throughout the United States dropout rates are lowest in small schools and tend to rise with the size of the school.

We cannot forget, either, that many children come from homes where parents are treated impersonally in large plants or stores or, if marginal, must spend hours receiving impersonal attention from doctors in overcrowded clinics and relief workers in overworked agencies.

If you are a "nobody," then you can make yourself a "somebody" by being obnoxious. There may be some link to note in the fact that Hell's Angels ride the roads of the state most enamored of computerized schools. A key educational task, then, is to devise educational arrangements under which every boy and girl can be a valued member of a continuing face-to-face group. There are many ways in which this can be done: we can build smaller schools, break big schools into house units, launch many special programs, expand the range of cocurricular activities. At the very least we can stare down the enthusiasts who think social problems can be solved by supermarket education dished out in monstrous "educational parks."

Different Emphasis

Another causal factor is that as the educational requirements for entry occupations go up and up, the junior high school student who cannot take the pressure to get ready for college, sees less and less value in the school he attends. Occupationally, it leads nowhere. He sees it as preparatory (for what?); terminal for nothing.

Let us study closely the attitudes of the youngsters with low achievement motivation, the boys and girls who will drop out, the ones who find more glory in "going grease" than in any adult-approved motivation. Here we note two qualities which pose problems for schools: (a) they are not motivated by future gratifications; and (b) they place little value on individuality.

One could well argue that they ought not to be that way, that we should do something to prevent such an outcome. Perhaps we should. (There is a legitimate value issue which can be argued; the author believes that people have a right to live with emphasis on the present if they wish and he has enough nonconformity in him to defend conformity if it is freely selected.)

Regardless of that, however, we have no tried-and-true program which would turn all children into future-oriented self-actualizers. Ergo, the youngsters, with their values and inclinations, are with us. That is a fact many school people have tried to ignore. With pride in our own values, we vaunt programs that inculcate personal uniqueness and organize instruction for distant goals.

Difficult as it is to question precious beliefs and long-admired practices, we must do so. We have grown comfortable, for example, with the classroom procedures which call for children and adolescents to work long periods of time gathering information for reports which are then presented to a class for discussion. Teachers, who value the self-purposing and creative young people, will praise, as a matter of course, the stellar classroom performer who exemplifies exactly those qualities.

The Pendulum

In every class, and especially in junior high schools, there are some boys and girls who hang back, who do not enter discussions, which they leave for those who "talk smart." Without giving the matter too much thought we assume that those young people we praise will serve as models of identification for their classmates, whom we surmise hunger for approval.

In schools serving underprivileged areas, we consider class reactions to these strategies as problems in discipline. Yet, is it not equally possible that by adopting routines which go against the grain of many young people, we are really increasing their alienation from school? Methods which do not respect the behavioral inclinations of students fly in the face of our value for individualizing instruction every bit as much as does refusal to take into account the differences in intellectual ability.

Observations such as the above are too often taken as implying a sweeping reversal of instructional trends. The argument goes that if an author says that "democratic" procedures do not work well with the alienated segments of our youth, then he means we must use autocratic procedures. The facts are thus utilized to bolster an all-or-none approach, one way or another.

What we are saying here is that incontestable realities indicate that our current procedures in junior high schools simply are not reaching significant numbers of students. It is equally uncontestable that they *are* effectively reaching many more. The solution, then, on the one hand, calls for retention and improvement of those practices for those whom they benefit; on the other hand, there is clear need to find some way to meet the needs of those who are being alienated.

How can this be done? One possibility is for teachers to individualize instruction or subgroup classes so that different processes can be geared to the psychological needs of the children or young people. Let the self-propelling pupils work in their own ways creatively to reach long-range goals; give the self-doubters the security of definite assignments. A second possibility is to group together the now alienated youth and have teachers work with them intensively to develop appropriate approaches.

We can no longer afford to deal with educational problems by swings of the pendulum. We should know by now that any approach if applied to all children alike will be bad for some. There is no solution but to deal with each boy or girl in terms of his or her characteristics understood in depth. This is especially the case at the junior high school level, where individual differences of all sorts are most visible.

PART 4

Curriculum for the Middle School

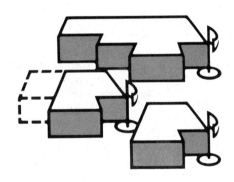

Curriculum Planning Priorities
for the Middle School

CONRAD F. TOEPFER, JR. *

THE MIDDLE SCHOOL concept continues to draw increasing attention from curriculum planners as a means to improve education for emerging adolescents in the middle grades of the American public school. As with any innovation, there is real concern to separate "faddism" from carefully planned instructional improvement. A serious problem centers on the persistent failure in most states to develop preservice teacher education programs for the middle grades. While some states are moving in this direction, the primary means to improve teacher skills and instructional programs in the middle grades will continue to reside in curriculum planning efforts of local districts through staff development and in-service education projects.

As school districts continue to reorganize middle school programs, they must avoid the pitfall of merely offering "old wine in new bottles." This dilemma can best be averted by developing systematic curriculum planning projects which: (a) involve staff and community in defining new objectives and directions for the middle grades; and (b) encourage the professional staff to develop new programs, write new curricula, and develop the instructional skills necessary to improve learning for students in the reorganized middle schools.

The fact that such effective change will take time, effort, and adequate fiscal underwriting must be squarely faced if improved programs for middle grades students are to be achieved. Unfortunately, many districts are opting a mere reorganization of the grades contained in the so-called middle school buildings and looking for an "add water and stir" phenomenon in hopes of achieving instant middle school success. Visits to districts entering upon such carpet-bagging efforts invariably bear witness to such results as disgruntled teachers, bored students, and a frustrated community which sees little evidence of improved learning, skill development, or self-concept in its children. In some situations, districts have already thrown off this flimsy mantle and moved back to older organizational patterns in the middle grades. However, an increasing number of school districts are utilizing the middle school movement in a concerted and realistic effort to reorganize and improve the quality of the educative experience for students in the middle grades.

The purpose of this piece is to identify

* *Conrad F. Toepfer, Jr., Associate Professor of Education, State University of New York at Buffalo*

> *The most effective redefinition of programs for emerging adolescents in the middle grades can be found in those districts where such efforts have been characterized by the earmarks of sound curriculum planning.*

a few of these programs and to specify why these approaches continue to have successful results. The focal consideration here is to synthesize those guidelines which may serve as a curriculum planning basis for schools seeking to improve their own middle grades programs.

A Rationale

One fact must be clarified before proceeding further. There is no suggestion here that the mere reorganization of any set of middle grades into a single program can provide realistic improvement of instruction. In the abstract, a fifth through eighth grade program has no intrinsic advantage over sixth through eighth, seventh through ninth, or other combination of grades. What the middle school concept can offer is an opportunity to reorganize a program based upon the localized capabilities of emerging adolescent learners. In some communities, maturational profiles may recommend a particular combination of grades which brings together the greatest number of emerging adolescents with a common range of skills, capacities, and needs as human beings and learners.

While medical evidence confirms national lowering of the age of pubescent maturation, the exact impact of such data must be determined at the local district level. With the identification of such local data, reorganization plans can then realistically be undertaken. Such efforts in virtually all of the nationally recognized middle school programs have included early strength and need assessment projects. It follows that effective curriculum improvement efforts can be undertaken only when local data reflect those areas in which current programs for emerging adolescents are successful as well as other areas in need of substantial improvement.

While such efforts will take time, they invariably bear great savings of both time and monies over poorly defined projects which intuitively assume needs for improvement. This frequently occurs when districts move quickly into a rapid surface reorganization of their middle grades. Staff teams are sent to visit various lighthouse middle schools with national reputations. Excitement far too often leads districts to conclude, "That's great! Let's adopt it back home." Few such efforts succeed for the simple reason that the characteristics of the students and community and the needs for improvement back home are rarely ever the same as circumstances in the lighthouse districts. At best, they waste time and money and result in an adoption of programs doomed to failure because they were implemented without identification of local district needs. However, where districts have taken the time to identify local student characteristics and district needs, realistic educational improvement has usually been realized.

Visitations to districts which have developed programs to meet needs similar to your own are most helpful. Evaluation should be made as to what aspects of the lighthouse programs can be adapted to help meet the areas of improvement identified in your local district. Seeking areas for *adaptation* to local needs rather than mass *adoption* of grandiose programs from afar can result in local district improvement of a most significant degree. Curriculum planning efforts to provide for such change must involve the staff and community to develop a basis of support which far surpasses a level of administrative enthusiasm. Again, the number of middle school programs which disappear when the innovating building administrator leaves, graphically indicates an inadequate staff understanding of, and support for, the program. It is important to contrast these situations against those which continue to flourish after the administrator guiding the original project moves on. It is this test of grass roots support which separates the instances of systematic improvement of programs for the middle grades from abortive efforts at surface change.

Lighthouse Programs

The instances which are cited in this section have persisted and flourished in their districts because they evolved through effective curriculum planning efforts on a sufficiently broad base of staff and community involvement. Each situation has developed upon a basis of planning which can be helpful to other districts seeking improvement in their particular area of emphasis.

Upper St. Clair, Pennsylvania. Both the Boyce and Fort Couch schools have developed a unique means to group middle grades youngsters in highly appropriate settings for learning and personal development. Working from a base of true multiage grouping, this program moves students into different student teams as they experience maturational or intellectual advancement, or a combination of both factors. The groupings take advantage of findings of a local study performed by the Pittsburgh Children's Hospital[1] and the five classifications of development by Tanner.[2] The humane emphasis of this program is complemented by amazing results in both intellectual growth of students as well as positive self-concept.

Where individual cases with parental support merit, possibilities exist for grouping sixth with eighth year students, of advancing students with intellectual and maturational skills to high school in as few as two years, or retaining socially mature eighth year students in the middle school for an additional semester or year by bringing them an enriched program. This program continues to stand out as one of the most effective grouping programs based upon medical and psychological data. Certainly, districts seeking to provide flexibility and responsiveness in grouping should continue

to look to this program as a source of ideas and practices viable for adaptation.

Decatur, Alabama. Among the most interesting of successes in the Oak Park and Brookhaven Schools is the mainstreaming of students with learning disabilities into the regular middle school program.[3] The architecture of the schools allows for small enclaves of sixth through eighth grade students in pod arrangements. Interdisciplinary teams in these pods are serviced by special education teachers who work with the teams to plan integrated learnings for the special education youngsters. This program has developed such effectiveness over the past three years that it was virtually impossible for an external accreditation team to identify the learning disability students in a three-day visitation.

Special learning needs of these youngsters have been accommodated through individualized instruction opportunities in learning resource centers and library-instructional media areas. The utilization of these facilities by all students has given a degree of anonymity and personalization to these activities for the special education students. The effectiveness of the program in the general education area has supported similarly effective learning experiences in the exploratory and activity phases of curriculum. Most encouraging is the positive attitude of these students toward school, their peers, and their personal progress. These schools continue to provide excellent examples of how youngsters with such disabilities can be helped to achieve personal and intellectual growth in an integrated setting with the rest of the school population at large.

Logansport, Indiana. The Logansport Community School Corporation has achieved unusual success in its efforts to develop teacher-student-made learning materials in the Columbia Middle School. The project has

[1] Donald Eichhorn. "The Boyce Medical Study." *The Emerging Adolescent Learner in the Middle Grades.* Multi-media Kit. Springfield, Massachusetts: Association for Supervision and Curriculum Development and Educational Leadership Institute, 1973.

[2] J. M. Tanner. *Growth at Adolescence.* Second edition. Oxford: Blackwell Scientific Publications, 1962.

[3] Robert Bumpus and Margaret Vann. "An Innovative Approach to Special Education in the Middle School." *Dissemination Services on the Middle Grades.* Springfield, Massachusetts: Educational Leadership Institute, Vol. 6, No. 1, September 1974.

been piloted in the Columbia School in hopes of being able to extend it into the other middle schools of the city as interest develops. Faculty support and enthusiasm for the project have continued to increase. Instructional material budgets for the school have been reorganized to maintain a supply of text materials primarily for reference with other monies reallocated to duplicating and production facilities, materials, and supportive personnel. Teacher reactions to the writing of resource units, instructional guides, and specific curriculum guides have been reinforced by the exciting learning activities which have been organized from the materials. The instructional materials are produced in low-cost fashion with the materials being usable for a maximum of three years. The need to develop new materials, update present ones, and support new concepts and directions has caused curriculum development to be a dynamic process in this setting. Student input and participation in developing materials and programs have also been cited as a significant gain. Districts interested in moving into this area of teacher participation in curriculum writing should examine this continuing program in Logansport.

Dewitt, New York. The Jamesville-Dewitt Middle School is an excellent example of how cooperative team planning and teaching can articulate the instructional experience for students across the range of subject offerings. This has been implemented within the physical setting of a house or school-within-a-school plan with great success. The house plan has organized enclaves of students and teachers in a reduced physical setting, and has provided a basis to help students make a positive adjustment to the program of the middle school. Cooperative team planning with the support of counselors and other pupil personnel specialists has made delivery of special help as immediate as possible through better teacher referral. Sharing of information about students among team members has helped in defining and extending appropriate instructional approaches to those students in need of a particular kind of help. The results of this program have been confirmed through the school's strong commitment of recording pupil growth data. Such data have also been the basis for redefining existing instructional programs to meet areas of learning needs not accommodated by earlier programs. Districts considering team and house plan departures should examine this program and its results before finalizing local staff or facility plans.

While hosts of other outstanding programs could be enumerated, the purpose in citing the foregoing four is threefold. First, each situation has developed an ongoing program over a period of time which has the commitment and enthusiasm of a large majority of staff members. Second, broader areas of improvement for emerging adolescents have been provided within which subject and other concerns have been improved. Each of these schools boasts outstanding programs in content areas. The excellence of their programs in subject areas could not have grown without their unique success in the broader areas cited in each instance. These schools have developed their unique success in areas which too many districts overlook in their haste to get into more narrow academic and content areas in and for themselves. Third, each of these situations has developed its success through a careful program of systematic curriculum planning on a continuing basis. It is this critical ingredient which is viewed as necessary to identify and organize means to improve middle grades programs at the local level.

Guidelines

The following guidelines have been drawn from those elements consistent in the four exemplary situations described as well as a number of other lighthouse middle school projects throughout the country. They are offered as important for districts seeking to launch middle school projects to bring about effective and ongoing improvement for their emerging adolescent populations.

1. Curriculum improvement in the mid-

dle grades of a school district must be undertaken only after a careful identification of how proposed changes will affect elementary and high school programs. Such changes in the middle school must be thought of as macrocosmic rather than microcosmic since they will have critical impact on the articulation of the local kindergarten through twelfth grade curriculum program. Unless the elementary program makes its own changes to prepare learners for planned departures in the middle school, the vital articulation of the K-12 program is only further confused and weakened. Likewise, the nature of the high school experience must be re-thought in terms of how it will build upon rather than thwart or contradict the proposed innovative changes in the middle school.

2. The objectives of projected changes in middle grades programs, as well as means to assess their projected improvements, should be carefully specified before launching the innovations. It is important that such means be able to measure both areas of success as well as needs for continuing improvement before the middle school innovation is inaugurated. Districts where middle school projects have flourished have invariably utilized such means to validate how the innovative programs in the middle grades have or have not improved upon previous programs. On the other hand, the vast majority of districts which have moved prematurely into hastily-defined middle school reorganizations have found that failure to define objectives has lessened their capability to determine the actual successes of the changes. In such situations, it is virtually impossible to validate objectively the degree of improvement which such innovations may actually have promoted.

3. Objectives of proposed changes in middle grades should be stated in terms of characteristics of the emerging adolescent population as defined in the local school-community setting. This process of local identification is a necessary step for planning means to improve instruction in the middle grades. Districts utilizing this procedure concur that it provides a frame of reference

In the early 1960's mounting dissatisfaction with the discontinuity of elementary and secondary schools and the resultant problems of children in moving from level to level, along with widespread criticism of schooling in general, and the search for innovations and alternatives created a receptive climate for middle school proposals and reorganizations.

against which they can validate the effects of specific innovations in terms of local emerging adolescent learner needs.

4. The proposed innovation in the middle grades must then be related to a curricular rationale to identify how it will achieve its purpose in terms of the three aforementioned guidelines. This, then, initiates a curriculum plan to implement the innovation as a realistic improvement. This curricular rationale should identify the sequence of tasks necessary to move forward in subsequent planning and implementation of the innovation. The development of the curriculum plan should identify both a time schedule for designing and implementing the innovation as well as the kinds of staff development experiences necessary to prepare staff to initiate the program. In organizing the curriculum plan, the role of such in-service activities as workshops and summer programs should become apparent. Means to evaluate the project should also be identified in determining the curriculum plan.

The sequential completion of the guidelines (1 through 4) makes the final task of designing an administrative vehicle to expedite and support middle grades instructional improvement largely one of facilitation and monitoring. Greater confidence of the staff and a sense of ownership in the program, as well as credibility and understanding by the local community, usually accrue from the experiences implied in the guidelines. Likewise, the enthusiasm of the staff members and their preparation to enter the project with skills and readiness from staff development experiences give a greater promise of success in meeting the objectives of the middle school innovation.

All that can be learned from the history of the theory and practice of systematic curriculum planning should point to the following. The most effective redefinition of programs for emerging adolescents in the middle grades can be found in those districts where such efforts have been characterized by the earmarks of sound curriculum planning. For districts not to launch such efforts on these bases seems tragic since the track record of such hasty efforts is quite dismal. If the redefinition of better programs for emerging adolescents is worth the effort, there appears to be every reason to organize such projects with the highest predictability for success. As you consider the middle school departures collected in this volume, then, examine them not only in terms of the programs themselves, but also what it would take for successful planning and adaptation in your own district and circumstances. ☐

EL 31 (3): 230-32; December 1973
© 1973 ASCD

Your Middle School Must

THE term "middle school" has suddenly become a part of our ever-growing educational jargon. Much like the terms "individualized instruction," the "needs of children," and the "open school," the concept of the "middle school" has a variety of meanings to different people. Students in "middle schools" vary in age from 10 to 14, and are grouped in several ways for clustering students.

The Madison, Wisconsin, schools group the students by grades in school, ranging from sixth grade students to eighth grade students. Another area school near Madison chose the grades 4 through 6 and termed itself a "middle school." Other schools in the Madison area have clustered students from grades 5 through 8 and grades 6 through 8 into a "middle school" structure.

The McFarland Community Schools group children nine years of age to twelve years of age into one school, which has now become known as a "middle school" primarily because students attend the "middle school" midway during their schooling.

The manner of clustering students is far less significant than the program available to students. Students older or students younger could very easily be incorporated into the "middle school," providing an appropriate program is designed for those students. The success of a "middle school," or any school, does not depend entirely on the age range of students; much of the success depends on the program provided by the staff and the school district.

Some 60 years ago, at the onset of the junior high movement, three needs were seen for students of the pre-teenage period of development:

1. Something different from self-contained classrooms with people trained in special subject areas, especially in the fields of science, math, and the related arts

2. Exploratory courses to help students decide on a more concentrated high school program

3. Adult guidance to help the child understand himself and to understand something about his potential.

What has resulted from the junior high movement is a "mini" high school program including such things as competitive sports and organizations based on high school students' needs.

Have a Revised Program!

DONALD E. BARNES*

The name "middle school" means nothing without a thorough program. The R & D Center at the University of Wisconsin, Madison, provided a model for McFarland Community Schools.

The Conrad Elvehjem School in McFarland could easily absorb students from grades 7 and 8 into the existing program by means of extending the program, using the same concept established for the younger students. The basic model used in McFarland is adapted from the model established by the Research and Development Center at the University of Wisconsin in Madison. The model is termed "Individually Guided Education/Multi-Unit School-Elementary (IGE/MUS-E). The model is now being extended into the upper grades to grade 12. When this model is properly implemented the clustering of students by grades or age levels will have little or no significance. The necessities will be well-trained staff members, sufficient materials, and appropriate facilities. The education of the youngsters will be continuous, progressive, and meaningful.

The model for IGE has been successful in elementary schools throughout the nation, and will be successful for "middle schools" and high schools, if the schools follow the suggestions of the R & D Center. The model is based on seven components:

1. An organization for instruction

2. A model for instructional programming for individual students

3. A model for developing measurement tools and evaluation procedures

4. Curriculum materials, related statements of instructional objectives, and criterion-referenced tests and observation schedules

5. A program for home-school communications

6. Facilitative environments in the school building

7. Continuing research and development to generate knowledge and to produce test materials and procedures.

Material for training staff members is available through the Research and Develop-

* Donald E. Barnes, Principal, Conrad Elvehjem School, McFarland, Wisconsin

Photo courtesy of the author
Learning stations enhance individualized instruction.

ment Center and through many departments of public instruction throughout the nation. The model may be adapted to local situations; however, caution must be given to those who deviate from the model to any great extent.

One unique factor helped the Research and Development Center with the implementation of the IGE concept: the Center developed curricular programs to enhance the concept. The Wisconsin Design for Reading Development is one such program. The Wisconsin Design includes Word Attack, Reference Skills, Study Skills, and Comprehension. Continuous progress for each student is ensured because of pre- and post-testing along with a record-keeping system. Tests are scored by a computer and recorded on an easy-to-read label for each child's McBee card.

Developing Mathematical Processes is a mathematics program being developed by the Research and Development Center and soon to be published. Student interest is high because students learn the concept by "doing" and the concept is then transferred to the abstract.

The R & D Center has other programs available, or soon to be available. McFarland has been part of the program development for the two programs mentioned. R & D Center programs used in the McFarland

IGE/MUS-E schools have enhanced the individualization of instruction.

The concept of IGE provides an opportunity to offer nongraded instruction to multiage clusters of students. The organizational structure finds an age span of three years in one unit. The current structure is four units; Unit I (kindergarten-grade 1), Unit II (grades 2 and 3), Unit III (grades 4 and 5), and Unit IV (grade 6). The structure could change at any time and would be extended to include grade 7, then grade 8, and on into the high school. Unit lines are not tight and can be flexible, with children attending classes in two different units within one day.

Potential for the extension of this type of structure is endless and is now being explored by the Research and Development Center in Madison. The concept of IGE in the multi-unit organization provides an opportunity to try many innovations: multiaged instruction, team teaching and team planning, continuous progress, youth tutoring, differentiated staffing, and working closer with teachers in the related arts area.

The "middle school" concept has provided educators with an opportunity to correct the errors of 60 years of junior high school development. To change the name of the approach from junior high to "middle school" affords the opportunity to make changes faster.

Universities throughout the nation should recognize that professional staff members need to be trained for the "middle school" level as a single entity. The present approach of borrowing staff members trained for elementary school or high school has been inadequate. The former bring the atmosphere of the elementary school to the "middle school," and high school teachers force "mini" high school programs upon the pre-teenage child.

A magic cutoff age has never been determined and should never become a factor. A continuous program of individualized instruction, based on individual students' progressing and developing at different rates, is drastically needed. The focus needs to be on the curriculum offering rather than on the organizational structure. □

EL 31 (3): 225-27; December 1973

Why the Middle School Curriculum Vacuum?

JAMES DiVIRGILIO*

Will supporters of the middle school be able to create a new instructional program congenial to today's preadolescents? Some efforts in this direction are noted.

THE middle school movement has engaged the imagination of educators throughout the country. Advocated as institutions unique and stimulating for preadolescents, middle schools are expected to rectify programs in which traditional junior high schools were ineffective. Under this new approach, no longer are preadolescents to be subjected to highly sophisticated adolescent-oriented activities, interscholastic athletics, and senior high instructional methods. No longer should pressures unsuited for students in early adolescence be perpetuated.

We have an opportunity to establish a new type of school. This new institution is to be sensitive to the growth and development needs of youngsters going through a strenuous period of physical, social, and emotional change. Literature about the middle school movement abounds, yet seldom is anything suggested regarding curriculum development. Of all the changes advocated for the middle school, the greatest vacuum exists in the area of appropriate curriculum development.

The changes that have been made in middle schools are in such areas as clubs, athletics, socials, and general school environment. These elements were less difficult to change and could be instituted with the least administrative effort. Yet the middle school movement would fall short of the goals its advocates most strongly desire unless one of the most frequent recommendations found in professional literature, the use of interdisciplinary teams, is implemented. In order for these teams to be effective, a revision of the curriculum commonly utilized is necessary. Currently the practice is to continue curriculum programs as they existed in the elementary fifth and sixth grades and the junior high seventh and eighth grades and to incorporate these programs into a middle school setting. This being so, it is apparent to educators interested in middle school growth that more effort is needed in projecting and organizing a curriculum that will enhance the further development of young people of middle school age.

* James DiVirgilio, Assistant Director of Secondary Education, Howard County Public Schools, Columbia, Maryland

Local School Efforts

Changes in middle school curriculum, where these have taken place, have largely been limited to local attempts to produce learning units facilitating cooperation between disciplines. These learning units were produced by teachers who were performing other duties at the same time. Consequently there were limitations as to what could be accomplished. The following examples show the awareness that faculty members have of the need to produce a program that will enable them to fulfill the purposes of the middle school.

Example: At Hammond Middle School in Howard County, Maryland, a nongraded interdisciplinary team developed a unit titled "The Assembly Line." The purpose of this unit is to help students understand concepts and practices related to production and sales.

Disciplines Involved: Social Studies, Language Arts, Science, Art, Home Economics, and Industrial Arts.

Project Goal: To make Snowmen (stuffed pillows) using the assembly line approach.

Procedures: Involved 130 students, heterogeneously grouped. Assembly line set up in pod. Students explored types of job opportunities, interviewed, and filled in applications. Company officers decided on by group. Officers placed students in jobs. Types of jobs included: salesmen, advertising and public relations, stuffers, gluers, sewers, inspectors, distributors, and foremen. Product was marketed.

The project took planning and preparation time, production time, and follow-up time. In two weeks, students had experienced not only the broad concepts of economics but also opportunities to practice skills in written and oral communication, interpersonal relations, and decision making. Resource people from the community assisted in the unit. Students analyzed the process and particularly the type of job they performed. Though many of these efforts are quite noteworthy, no attempts are being made to utilize them beyond the school in which they were developed.

Middle school students respond to projects in which they may interact as social beings.

National Curriculum Projects

While teachers and students are producing locally made materials, curriculum programs in this area have been developed by federal projects, universities, and commercial companies and are constantly being marketed. These nationally organized curriculum attempts such as BSCS Biology, AAAS Science, and Nebraska English have resulted in designs limited to the narrow confines of a particular discipline. Use of such programs dictates a school organized by disciplines. For example, to place a science program in a middle school that requires the science teacher to perform in the area of science to the exclusion of other disciplines breaks down the relationships sought in the interdisciplinary approach.

With a discipline-organized curriculum the opportunities for a team of teachers to meet with a common group of students, diagnose their needs, and prescribe accordingly become very limited. In an interdisciplinary-organized school a curriculum organized by subject disciplines dictates methods by which class groups of 30 students form the instructional pattern even when 120+ students are assigned to a "team" of four teachers. Because of these limitations, many middle schools are reorganizing into disciplinary teams shifting students period by period.

Admittedly teachers in this setting can use a greater variety of teaching strategies than can their interdisciplinary counterparts using the same traditional curriculum. The effect is that no group of teachers has a student for more than one class period. Instead the pitfall common to the junior high school becomes the pattern and the middle school then loses one of the ingredients strongly desired by its advocates. The preadolescent in need of daily guidance by all who are responsible for his school environment soon realizes that the major portion of his school day is no different than it was in any other school he attended. The vacuum that exists is the lack of an instructional program that encourages the best use of interdisciplinary relationships.

In conclusion, the middle school movement is in need of an in-depth, well funded project to produce a suitable curriculum. Such a curriculum would contain units which encourage administrators and teams to capitalize on all of the advantages of the interdisciplinary organization that is strongly recommended for the middle school. Recognition must be made of those disciplines or units within a single discipline that can most effectively be accomplished only when approached as a separate discipline. Thus the middle school curriculum, like the middle school organization, will utilize the best of two worlds, a combination of disciplinary and interdisciplinary relationships. It will contain those elements which permit a diagnosis of each student's mastery of basic fundamentals as well as encourage a wide variety of opportunities for learning experiences relevant to the student's world.

A good middle school curriculum is not one that results in memorizing content. Instead it offers the learner alternatives of experiences. The content should be the vehicle through which the learner develops his fundamental skills and concepts of life. The content of the middle school curriculum then consists of the high interest materials, not necessarily logically organized, which will help to produce a student who is anxious to get to high school to investigate further. ☐

... the middle school curriculum, like the middle school organization, will utilize the best of two worlds, a combination of disciplinary and interdisciplinary relationships.

EL 27 (7): 578-81; March 1970
© 1970 ASCD

Rationale for

CURRICULAR innovation would seem to us to be the most cogent rationale for the development of the middle school organization. We believe that the purposes of education appropriate to the emerging adolescent are so varied and so broad that a reorganization of instructional practices into a systematic plan for such an innovation is necessary. We hold that the optimum growth of every student, and the balance between the physical, social, emotional, and intellectual areas of development of the pupil, can be achieved within such a system.

Many rationales for the middle school place a considerable stress upon those facets and purposes which are *unique* to the middle school, while accepting some facets and purposes of both elementary and secondary school purposes. *The primary emphasis in the middle school program should be upon the total personalization of purposes and standards for the pupils in such a program.*

Purposes of the Middle School

Differential education derives from different personal developmental needs. The development of a plan for instruction to take into account the extreme range of individual differences evident in these groups of emerging adolescents is an absolute essential for the middle school. These differences in individual students and in their stages of maturation must be reflected in the purposes, methods, and objectives in education for emerging

adolescents in the middle schools. Different youngsters may have different personal needs when attending a school. They certainly will have differing sets of values due to background, intellect, physical development, and other related concerns. With this focus, the use of normative standards and grade level rankings is less appropriate than individual progress reports.

The major purposes of personalization in the middle school are derived from the three areas of general education, learning skills, and exploratory experiences. General education which all children should experience is and should remain the central focus of education in the middle school, with specific content developed as necessary to support this area. Extensive effort in seeking an appropriate balance among the areas of the total curricular and educational patterns is necessary.

The stress on general education requires a reassessment of the various subject matter areas with a view to more effective structuring of learning experiences. An emphasis on development of key concepts and modes of inquiry is also recommended. Less emphasis on the learning of facts as a product of learning is necessary with this concern for appropriate modes of inquiry. Further, interdisciplinary approaches and a synthesis of content are recommended to counteract fragmentation, and to render possible a greater applicability and use of new concepts and structures.

Instruction in the Middle School

THOMAS E. CURTIS *
WILMA W. BIDWELL

Learning skills sufficient to enable the student to become an independent learner should be assessed and emphasized to the point of mastery. These are the skills which the pupil utilizes in mastering the higher, more abstract levels of cognitive processes. Full utilization of the learning resources center would require appropriate general learning skills. Skill in the application of fundamental tools such as reading, writing, and arithmetic is necessary to enable the individual pupil to go beyond his current knowledge, and to achieve mastery of library techniques, technological devices, and a range of study methods. Because of the extremely uneven development in these areas of skill, pupils must be allowed to progress at their own optimal rates in the mastery of such learnings.

The third area of focus in the middle school curriculum is exploration. Exploration is the learning which takes place when the pupil exercises his own initiative in seeking experiences in which his interest arises from his own unique personal needs, desires, or purposes. It is appropriate in any subject area, and it is essential that the school systematically and regularly free the pupil for some set portion of time to develop his unique talents, both in areas within the regular curriculum, and in those areas not ordinarily covered in a traditional school program. Exploration as a concept derives from the purposes and initiative of the individual pupil rather than from the purposes of society; and,

as such, it is crucial among the educational purposes of the middle school.

Instructional Imperatives

The changes in instructional demands inherent within the above-named purposes will require different capabilities of teachers. Teachers will need to become, first, diagnosticians of learning needs; second, resource persons to guide instruction; and third, assessors of the effectiveness of learning experiences and activities in the achievement of special purposes for individual students.

To perform the role of diagnostician, the teacher must ascertain the level of development of a pupil on a number of different dimensions in learning within the particular subject matter with which the teacher is concerned. A more specific type of evaluation will be required than those with which we are currently functioning. Specific learning processes and particular problems within given subject areas will have to be sequenced in such a way that a student's progress can be plotted on a cluster of related learning tasks. With specific learning processes evaluated, the teacher can then begin to diagnose the status and learning of the youngster, and to prescribe the next steps to be selected for

* Thomas E. Curtis, Associate Professor of Education, and Wilma W. Bidwell, Associate Professor of Curriculum and Instruction; both at the State University of New York at Albany

forward movement along the learning path for the pupil.

The teacher must develop a thorough understanding of the school's curriculum development, learning sequences, scope, and syntheses possible between subject areas in order to best guide pupils in their growth. In determining next steps for individual learners, there must be a variety of opportunities for possible learning experiences so that pupils can select different opportunities according to their varying growth needs. The teacher must know what resources are available to students to facilitate pupil growth and to further develop capabilities. In other words, the staff must develop viable alternatives from which the pupil may choose to provide the most effective learning experiences in terms of individual needs. Staff differentiation and in-service education may become essential aspects of an organizational framework to implement these goals most effectively.

The teacher must study the efficacy of these methods and resources for different types of purposes and different types of youngsters. Teachers must understand the implications for curriculum and instructional decision making and must be prepared to work with students individually to assist each in his progress toward achieving the educational objectives set for this comprehensive plan.

Teachers must be prepared to ascertain where each student is currently working and how he may proceed for continuous growth toward mutually accepted objectives. The variety of instructional acts, no matter what their modes, must be multiplied in order to achieve the desired purposes. Familiarity with unusual processes, modes of inquiry, structure of subject areas, and resources will be required. Nature of key concepts, generalizations, principles, and laws which create structure in parent disciplines must also be understood. Further, knowledge and ability to organize these so they are understandable and learnable by students are vital if the instructional practices in the middle school are to be most effective. □

EL 31 (3): 267-70; December 1973
© 1973 ASCD

When Students Choose and Use Independent Study Time

DOROTHY L. FISHER

Students develop confidence and poise through a Detroit middle school's built-in plan for decision making.

THE Region Seven Middle School has included in its organization several opportunities for *student choice* of *curriculum areas of learning.* Our staff feels strongly that students of grades 5 through 8 need experiences in making decisions. In today's world our young students are already making many decisions outside of school—and very serious decisions. These grades are no longer part of childhood in the "old" sense. Therefore, they need to learn to make decisions they will stand by; they need to feel they *can* make such decisions and that people will respect their choices. This confidence and poise will help them throughout their lives. Thus, we consider decision making an *essential* skill in "today's school."

There are many ways to give children opportunities for decision making. We have incorporated such opportunities in our organization. We have: set IST (Independent Study Time) each week, schoolwide IST

every Wednesday, and for our final session, student choice of a total plan of work.

To explain these terms:

Set IST. We have four *sets* of teachers, with four teachers in each set. Our students work with each set of teachers for *sessions* of eight weeks. Each set of teachers allows anywhere from two periods to ten periods a week for *Set IST.* Students, on the days that have IST for the set, use conference time to sign up for the one or two classes they wish to work in for the IST. They may choose rooms: to finish work, to enjoy a project they have started and want to continue, to work with the teacher on some part of the unit, or just because they like the class. Let us remember—if it's fun we can still learn! Signing up for IST does take time in the conference period, but students and staff members feel that the time is well worth it. At the end of conference, teachers exchange lists of students signing for the different rooms. In one set, all four conferences meet in the large cafeteria and the students move from teacher to teacher in signing up on the Set IST days.

Is there any teacher guidance? Certainly. Four teachers working with their set of about 125 students know them well, and can encourage and suggest wise choices for the students if it is necessary. In practice, our staff has found that 98 percent make wise choices and return to classes for help and to finish work on their own. Students *can* be trusted to want to learn if they feel it is *their* responsibility. The one or two who do not respond to independent choices would need strong guidance in any organization. Staff members, parents, and students strongly feel IST is a learning experience for students.

Schoolwide IST. To prepare our students for a choice of their total curriculum in our final session (described later), our staff initiated a half-day schoolwide IST. It proved so successful and so interesting to teachers and students that it was extended to

a full-day experience. Now every Wednesday our students report to classes they choose— two morning classes and two afternoon classes. They may choose any curriculum area in the school. This gives them the opportunity to work with teachers or in the curriculum areas they especially like, even when that room is not part of their working set. (As noted previously, every eight weeks our students move to another set of teachers —in this way they work with all of our teachers for eight weeks, one set at a time.) With schoolwide IST they can maintain a year-long activity if they wish to, and some do. Other students prefer a change of interest.

How do students sign up and what do teachers offer? These are the steps followed:

1. It was decided to do this in terms of

Photos courtesy of the author

Students are encouraged to balance their choices between classes they simply enjoy and classes that also sharpen their basic skills.

two weeks at a time, so when teachers and students sign up they are signing up for a two-week IST.

2. Two weeks ahead, teachers sign for all four periods indicating topics they will offer. Students look these over. They also may work on independent projects in a room rather than on what the teacher offers.

3. One week ahead students sign up in their conference rooms for their four periods. Only two students from each conference room may sign with a particular class each period unless the teacher gives an OK for more in his or her class.

4. By Friday of the week before the school-wide IST starts, each conference room sends the student sign-up set to the office. There students cut the sheet and staple all the choices of the same classes together—so that the names of all who choose each class would be stapled together These final lists are given to the teacher to check attendance in the room at a certain time.

Final Session. This session offers students a chance to plan their complete week's schedule. Our first year we had the session for two weeks and everyone found it so stimulating we extended this to four weeks the second year.

The organization for our final session requires time, but the personal interaction of staff and students, and the opportunity for students to make the decisions and changes of original plans, seem to make it essential. Efficiency might lead to shorter ways but the education and encouragement of opportunities for student experiences prompt us to continue this type of organization.

One to two months ahead teachers think through their curriculum and the type of interesting activities which would extend student growth in their curricular area. They think back to the unit and activities students enjoyed or requested. Thus teachers project their plans of work. We have found it best to schedule for Monday, Wednesday, and Friday, or Tuesday and Thursday each period of the day. We have two morning periods and two afternoon periods. A few teachers need a longer time than a period to do some of their activities, so we have established

that Tuesday and Thursday could be double periods; this means students would have four periods a week that way. They could have two long sessions to complete longer activities such as food preparation and out-of-school science trips.

Do teachers ever have a chance to work with students especially skilled or especially needing help? Yes—our staff has established some "closed" classes. These classes are closed except to students invited by the teacher to participate in them. Examples of these closed classes are: Research Skills by our Media teacher for our very able students, Glee Club, Basic Math for those who need strengthening, and Advanced Algebra for eighth graders who are able students. The students may take advantage of these invitations, or if there is a conflict of interest when the closed class is offered, it is left to the student to decide to accept or not. Again, in developing this session students are encouraged to think about their decisions, to balance their choices so they will have classes they enjoy, classes which will help them in their coming years, classes that will bring them help in basic skills, as well as classes that are fun.

It is reassuring to discover how intelligently fifth through eighth graders can do this and, as they do it, it is a joy to see their pride and their poise in being able to do a good job. This is also true for our very able students, our average students, and those who need much basic work. This development serves young people of all levels of ability.

Once teachers have made *their* plans of work, copies of the 18 plans are run off and posted in each room and the cafeteria. Students have about a week to look them over. After a schoolwide assembly to explain our final session, to discuss how to make choices, and to answer questions they have, students begin to make their individual plans of work, a form for which is provided.

Every conference room has some way to number everybody's sheet 1 to 30, then all sheets are sent to the *verification room*. The verification room is any available room in the building where we can verify all these plans

Independent study provides time to finish work, to continue projects, or to obtain help in difficult subjects.

of work. All staff members free, including the administrators, media center personnel, and career consultants, work with the students.

To ensure fairness and that it is a matter of luck as to which students have the first chance to have their plans of work verified, a number is drawn, and the students from each conference room whose plan has that number come for verification. When they have had their plans of work okayed another number is drawn and more students report to the verification room. No favoritism is shown and students can and do accept this well.

To verify the plans of work it is necessary to move around the room and sign students on the class sheets for each class the teacher is offering. When a class has 24 to 28 sign up, that class is closed. Thus the later numbers drawn find some of their classes

closed and must make second and even third choices. By having the students work with the staff, they continue to make the final decisions about their classes. This process takes three weeks since it cannot be done continuously but only as several of the staff members have time to do it. When it is done the class sheets are given to the teachers along with the final plan of work for their conference class. We make a carbon copy so the office can keep a file of these choices too.

Thus, with Set IST, Schoolwide IST on Wednesdays, and the Final Session, we provide continuing opportunities for experiences in decision making for *their* life for all of our students. This approach means much work but students, parents, staff members, and administrators evaluate it as worthwhile for practical education in today's school!

—DOROTHY L. FISHER, *Principal, Region Seven Middle School, Detroit, Michigan.*

EL 30 (3): 215-17; December 1972
© 1972 ASCD

Occupational Versatility:

KEY to careers

JOHN LAVENDER*

JEFF RAYMOND, an eighth grade student, enters the industrial arts shop at Chinook Junior High School in the Highline District. Jeff takes red notebook #12 from the bookcase. The notebooks are color-coded by period, with the color "red" signifying first period, and "12" being Jeff's student number. Today is the second day of the fall term, and of Jeff's first full year in shop after a nine-week session as a seventh grader.

In his notebook are the record sheets which Jeff will maintain during the term. Jeff knows he is responsible for selecting the area in which he wishes to work and for electing or designing the project he wishes to make. Jeff also knows he is to manage all his activities in the shop. These management responsibilities include his attendance record, his material purchases record, his planning records, his power equipment usage record, and his performance record.

The shop is a large single room with a team of three teachers available to the students. Eleven activity areas are available for Jeff to explore: woods, plastics, general industries, graphics, electricity/electronics, drafting, power, foundry, welding, cold metals, and career guidance. Notebook in hand, he wanders about looking at the brightly colored tool panels and the many project ideas displayed throughout the shop.

A 16-gauge sheet metal candlestick holder catches his eye. "My mother would like one of those, but I think she would like it a little taller," Jeff tells a girl looking at the same project. "I think I'll redesign it and make her one."

On his plan sheet, Jeff draws a sketch of the holder 12 inches high instead of the 10-inch height indicated on the shop plan. He then determines the procedural steps which he will follow, and he also calculates the total price of his project from the metals price list. Jeff asks Mr. Fowler to check his planning and then selects the material he is going to use.

After cutting and rolling the three pieces of metal to the desired shape, Jeff checks his plan. The next step is to cut an oval-shaped hole in each piece, which will require the use of an oxyacetylene torch. After using self-instructional materials for learning how to use the shears and forming rolls, Jeff knows he also must prepare himself to use the torch. He goes to the book on torch operation and reads the safety rules and operating pro-

* *John Lavender, Industrial Arts Consultant, Self Instructional Systems, Tacoma, Washington*

cedures. He looks at the loop films on how to light the torch and on how to cut metal with it. From the chart posted by the torch, he determines the pressures required. A ninth grader using the torch gives him some helpful advice. When Jeff believes he is ready, he fills in his power equipment record, indicating where he received his instructions, and asks Mr. Boe to check him out on the torch.

After his demonstration has been approved, Jeff then uses the torch to cut the three oval holes. When he is ready to weld his project, he goes through a similar self-instructional process.

Upon completion of his project, Jeff fills in the blanks on his performance record indicating the processes he used and the machines he operated. Jeff also completes a satisfaction index form on which he expresses how he felt about the work he did. Jeff knows that he is not working for a grade, but for the experience and the pride of accomplishment. The students in the program work independently or team together, without peer competition. The experience

Each student should learn to identify goals and to evaluate his own progress.

itself is the reward, and satisfaction comes from a job well done.

Choice of a Career

Looking back on his experience, Jeff thinks that he rather liked operating the oxyacetylene torch. It was hot and smoky, but he felt like an artist flowing the metal together with the flame. The burning was interesting too, but it surely took a steady hand. "What type of education is needed to be a welder," Jeff wonders, "and what kind of life does a welder live?"

Jeff looks at the two large boards in the career guidance area of the shop and he finds that the career of welding is colored green. The color-coding instructions tell him that "green" means post-high school training in the form of apprenticeship or technical school is necessary for this career. The directory also indicates there is a film he can watch on the welding profession, and a taped interview with a welder to which he can listen. After the film and tape are played, Jeff checks the apprenticeship requirements and the available technical programs in the Seattle area. This information, plus the experience of operating a torch, gives Jeff much of the background that he needs to analyze the welding profession.

This type of brief episode in Jeff's exploration of the industrial arts area at Chinook Junior High is repeated many, many times in the shop program. Jeff is learning how to function in the shop environment; he is learning to be responsible for all of his activities and to solve his problems himself. As the director of his own learning, there are many decisions he must make and be accountable for.

Many times, after completing his candlestick holder, Jeff selects the area in which he desires to work, chooses a problem he wishes to solve, develops a plan and a procedure for the solution, teaches himself the processes he needs, manufactures the project, and evaluates the results. Jeff has found his identity in the industrial arts environment and has developed the abilities to be self-sufficient, productive, and adaptable. He

Through career experiences, pupils become self-sufficient, productive, and adaptable.

has developed his own mode of operation and has become "Occupationally Versatile." He is ready for advanced or specialized training.

This is true career guidance at the exploratory level. The problems and questions are very real to the student as he initiates them. The solutions come about through student involvement in relevant situations. The degree of thinking often extends to, and sometimes beyond, the analysis level defined in Bloom's taxonomy. The key to such learning is the establishment of an environment where the student will be naturally motivated to learn—and responsible for his learning.

At the awareness and preparatory level, the following considerations must also receive attention. The learning method— where the student is responsible—should be consistent, but the content (what the stu-

dent is involved in) should be different and varied. The awareness level of career development should be integrated into the regular program and not be treated as a special program of study; it should be a natural aspect of all activities.

Goal must replace role at the preparatory level as the major emphasis. Skills, in terms of both quality and quantity, become significant. Each student should be able to identify what his own goals are and should also be able to evaluate how well he is doing in reaching these goals. This self-evaluation is the final aspect of career analysis which the student needs—"How well can I do what I want to do?" A student who has had worthwhile awareness, exploratory, and preparatory career experiences will likely know what he can do—and will do it well. □

EL 30 (8): 736-37; May 1973
© 1973 ASCD

Learning Centers-Stations-Places

CHARLOTTE ANN SPRINGFIELD*

"BOY, this sure was a fun way to learn," Ruth Ann exclaimed.

"I like learning this way better because my teachers help me a lot more than when they stood in front of the class and talked," said Peggy.

"Our school is different from the high school. They all have to use the same book and open to the same page during their classes," explained Fred.

These comments were made about learning "stations-centers-places." Peggy, Ruth Ann, and Fred, three students at Mebane Middle School, had expressed in their own words some of the reasons for using learning stations as one method of instruction in the classroom.

One Way To Individualize

Many professional educators believe that individualization is one way to "effective learning." Use of learning stations is a means to implement the concept of individualization in the classroom.

To illustrate this, let us suppose we are doing a unit on Australia. There are four objectives: (a) the students will name and describe the animals native to Australia; (b) the students will describe the physical land features of Australia; (c) the students will name the natural resources in Australia; (d) the students will describe the different types of life styles in Australia.

Now—how to individualize this unit through learning stations? First of all, pretest the students on the four objectives (it is important to pretest in order to evaluate the student's present knowledge of the unit). Second, set up learning stations for the objectives. Third, assign students to the learning stations based on pretest results. Students whose prior knowledge or understanding is sufficient to achieve a particular objective are not required to attend the learning station relating to that objective.

Going a little further, let us take the objective of naming and describing the animals native to Australia. To achieve this objective, it is necessary to be able to use the media center, that is, use the card catalog and encyclopedias. In most classes, some students do not have this skill, some need a review, while others are adept at it.

In order to let "the others" move forward, explore, extend experiences, and avoid boredom, the teacher may want to set up a skills learning station for some students on "how to use the media center." In this way,

* Charlotte Ann Springfield, Teacher, Mebane Middle School, Alachua, Florida

not everyone has to study this skill, only those who do not have it. By having different areas set up with objectives and skills, it is possible to organize learning activities to fit each child at his own pace.

More Time To Help

The teacher has more time to help, support, and guide students when he does not have to dictate to them and try to rule them. After an orientation on how to use learning stations, teachers can actually see the difference in the amount of increased time they have to devote to helping students learn.

To aid in the orientation of students, it is helpful to have explicit directions—either taped or written—in each classroom, ditto sheets for each child to keep, and a combined teacher-student week of learning how to use learning stations. In due course, there is freedom from wasted class time spent repeating instructions needlessly.

In addition, the learning station has all materials needed to complete the objectives, for example, a variety of textbooks, newspapers, magazines, art paper, paint and brushes, crayons, filmstrips and projectors, transparencies, overhead projectors, worksheets, charts, tapes, and recorders—in other words, anything to help the students learn the concepts. By having all these materials available to the students, the teacher no longer has to man an information booth. Therefore, cutting out time spent in locating materials in the classroom and in repeating instructions, the teacher becomes a teacher.

It does take time to prepare the learning stations so that they are valuable and attractive; but any worthwhile preparation is not easy, so why not prepare a method that frees class time? Once the job is done, everything is ready to go.

A Pleasant Style

Each child has a learning style that is best suited for him; and when a child receives instruction in a way compatible with his learning style, his experience is a pleasant one and pleasant circumstances are sought, not rejected.

Let us go back to Australia and its animals again and see how we can make this unit fun and valuable for each student. First of all, in setting up the learning stations, it is important to make them attractive. Bright colors, pictures, mobiles, bold letters—use anything to catch the student's attention. The classroom sets the tone for learning, so why not make it a happy place to learn?

Second, think of as many activities or ways as possible for the students to learn the objectives. The students can draw a mural of the animals and their habitats; make puppets of the animals; read textbooks, magazines, and newspapers; do research in the media center; watch films and filmstrips; write fictional stories or poems involving the animals; make up crossword puzzles about the animals; listen to a mini-lecture; play picture identification games, etc.

Communicate these activities to the students (usually written under the objective), and let them choose the ones they would like to do to achieve the objective. Thus, with a variety of projects and all the materials needed to complete these activities, the students have many avenues to explore and choose from.

One question frequently asked is, suppose the child chooses to draw all the time? Hopefully, a little guidance combined with the act of drawing or doing an experiment will arouse the curiosity of the student and eventually will lead him to participate in a multitude of learning experiences.

Learning stations are one method to be used in teaching. This approach is successful with some students, while others are "turned off." Therefore, it is important that teachers be cautioned not to make this the "only way" method, but rather to use it in connection with other techniques. If learning stations are used in this perspective, that is, as one method of helping students learn, both teachers and students may find in learning stations—whether skill building, exploratory, or reinforcing—the opportunities for more help and more individualization, all happening in an atmosphere of fun.   ☐

EL 29 (7): 621-26; April 1972
© 1972 ASCD

VALUES
CLARIFICATION
IN
JUNIOR HIGH SCHOOL

MILDRED W. ABRAMOWITZ*
CLAUDIA MACARI

Do I have to go to the streets to get changes?

Does it make any difference to our government what I do?

Does religion have any meaning for me?

Should I follow what my parents do in religion?

How can I make school more meaningful?

How can I make better use of weekends?

How do I know where to draw the line on a date?

What is there to talk about in my family?

Jack was a close friend. Now we pass each other without a word to say. What happened?

How can I get money to work for me instead of my working for it?

What should I believe about drugs? diet? eggs? meat? mercury?

How should I wear my hair? Should I grow a beard?

THESE are just a few of the questions young people are asking today, and, of course, they are not just for the young but for all of us.

If young people were to come to you

for help with these questions, could you answer them?

They are the big questions in our lives, and only we can answer them for ourselves. Schools have not been very helpful. They have not given us the tools to answer them. The *values clarification approach* is one attempt to give young people the tools to answer—a chance to shape their lives.

The Key Questions

Adolescents are living in a very confusing world where they must continually make choices regarding their attitudes and actions in politics, religion, work, school, leisure, love and sex, family, friends, spending of money, health, and personal taste. These are all areas of confusion and conflict for them, because things are changing so fast that they have great difficulty in looking to the past for the "proper" way to behave. They have few established models. They are asking questions; and as they weigh what their parents say and do, what their friends say and do, and what their teachers say and do, they find uncertainty, inconsistency, and even no answers at all to the key questions

* Mildred W. Abramowitz, Professor of Education, Brooklyn College, New York; and Claudia Macari, Assistant Principal, Niles Junior High School 118 Bronx, New York

Students are encouraged to take a stand on what they believe.

of their lives. They flounder for answers by themselves, and our schools have not been very helpful in developing the processes to help them get the answers.

Traditionally, schools have tried to impose values, or they have tried to ignore the whole problem, or they have said that it is not an area of their concern but that of parents and the church. Yet in this day of rapid change, adolescents are confronted with many different points of view, and they are then left to sort them out. The purpose of the values clarification approach is to give pupils experience in valuing to enable them to answer the questions that really concern them. It is important to pupils that schools are concerned with what they regard as personally important to them, as well as with their traditional role of passing on the achievements of the past.

Values are not readily transmitted, but they can be learned. If one accepts the idea that values cannot effectively be taught, but that they can be learned, one moves from moralizing and inculcating toward a process of value-clarification. Value-clarification involves a series of strategies which are not guilty of forcing one set of right values down the throats of all students. Instead, the process tends to raise issues, to confront the student with inconsistencies, and to get him to sort out his own values, in his own way, and at his own pace. The practice of this approach and the theory on which it is based

have been developed over a number of years by Louis Raths, Merrill Harmin, and Sidney Simon. A full presentation can be found in the book *Values and Teaching* [1] and in *New Strategies in Values Clarification.*[2]

In our school we are interested in values clarification teaching as one way to help our pupils know what they feel about what happens to them in the course of a day. We believe that thinking is accompanied by feeling, and we would like to experiment with ways of taking advantage of this so that pupils can be helped to answer the questions: Who am I? Where am I going? What do I care about? Is this what I want to do? What alternatives do I have? Which choice is wisest for me? We think that being able to answer such questions would make life more meaningful to our boys and girls, and in the process would help to make school a place where they would grow and where their lives would be affected.

Sidney Simon says that "it turns out that most people have very few values." [3] Values clarification teaching is based on the seven criteria for the determination of a value developed by Louis Raths. Raths' contribution was unique, in that he was not interested so much in the content of the value (whether materialistic or spiritual) but was interested in the process whereby a value came about. He said a value started with a belief you were proud of and were willing to affirm, where you had chosen it from alternatives with regard to possible consequences and free from outside pressure to choose any particular thing, and where you had taken action on this belief other than to talk about it and had done this in a regular pattern, not just at sporadic times. Value-indicators are people's beliefs, attitudes, morals, activities, interests, feelings, goals, and aspirations; but they are

[1] L. E. Raths, M. Harmin, and S. Simon. *Values and Teaching.* Columbus, Ohio: Charles E. Merrill Publishing Company, 1966.

[2] S. Simon *et al. Values Clarification: A Handbook of Practical Strategies for Teachers and Students.* New York: Hart Publishing Co., 1972.

[3] Sidney Simon. "Promoting the Search for Values." *Educational Opportunity Forum* 1 (4): 84; Fall 1969. Special issue on Psychological Humanistic Education. Albany: New York State Education Department.

not values unless they meet the seven criteria. We may have many value-indicators, which are certainly good things to have, but very few values.

The theory further states that people with very few values tend to be conforming, apathetic, inconsistent, and often very ambivalent, all of which seems quite sad when one realizes the extent to which values should guide a man's life. This argues strongly for the school's taking a more active part in the clarification of values. There are few areas in the affective domain about which there is so much talk and so little action as there is with values. The valuing process weaves together critical thinking and affective education in a functional and relevant program.

Our ideas, methods, and inspiration were given to us by Sidney Simon of the University of Massachusetts and his colleague, Howard Kirschenbaum, the director of Adirondack Mountain Humanistic Education Center. We attended several of their workshops and worked with five classes and ten members of our faculty during the school year 1970-71. This current school year (1971-72) we are conducting a teachers workshop in our own school during the school day, and we are also working with three classes for demonstration and practice purposes. One of these classes was with us

Values cannot effectively be taught, but they can be learned.

last year, and we are planning to continue with this class for a third year.

William W. Niles Junior High School is located in a disadvantaged area in the Bronx. The student body is 60 percent Puerto Rican and 40 percent Black, and the pupils are familiar with the problems of perpetual mobility, broken homes, absent fathers, drugs, and violence in the streets and in the home. Achievement is low in reading, writing, and oral expression. Admissions and discharges result in a one-third turnover in the course of a school year. Literacy in any language is a problem. The boys and girls are, on the average, more than two and a half years retarded in reading and in mathematics when they come to us from elementary school. The school is well thought of and well liked in the community because it has a concerned faculty that works hard at teaching and at establishing warm relationships with children and parents and to foster self-discipline so that teachers can concentrate on teaching.

Specific structured techniques have been designed to accomplish the goals of values clarification teaching. Some of these are described here.

Strategies

The strategies which were presented to our students were employed for the purpose of stimulating thinking and of making them aware of the processes of values clarification. Students were encouraged to take a stand on what they believed, declare it publicly, make their choice freely, and to act upon it. However, the right of the student to "pass" on any strategy was respected and protected. It is necessary to have the right not to say anything. Whatever was said by the student was accepted with no sign of condemnation, rejection, or ridicule. The task of not commenting or of controlling one's facial expressions is the most difficult of all. It is only in a free and relaxed atmosphere of mutual respect and acceptance that the pupils can express themselves and think about where they stand and how they feel and how they will act upon issues that affect their lives.

The following strategies are some examples of those used in our classes:

1. *I Love To Do.* Students were asked to write 20 things they love to do. (Incidentally, all written work is absolutely private and is only shared with others if the student wants to.)

The procedure that followed was:

1. Star the five things you love to do best of all.
2. Place a check after the things you love to do alone.
3. Place a cross after the things you love to do with other people.
4. Circle the things that cost you less than $3 to do.
5. Write the date of the last time you did each of these 20 things.

This strategy gives the student some insight into what is important to him. It reveals his needs for companionship or his lack of it, pleasures which may cost very little, and helps him to evaluate the way he spends his time.

2. *Alternative Search.* There are times when our students are stymied and frustrated by situations and incidents in their lives. They are overwhelmed by the feeling that they do not know where to go or how to act and that they inevitably have to bow to circumstances or fight without direction or reason. Students must be trained to examine a situation and consider all possible alternatives.

For example, the following problem is given to the students as a strategy for alternative search:

You are walking home and as you approach the building in which you live, you see a man and woman standing in a doorway. They are arguing loudly and violently. Suddenly the man pulls the woman by the hair and slaps her face, punches her in the eye. She screams again and again and calls for help.

Directions: Form a group of three people. Each person will say in turn one action he would take in this situation. One person will record what is being said. All answers are to be accepted without comment or criticism no matter how ridiculous or impossible they may seem. This is a way of brainstorming. Do not judge or evaluate the ideas given in this search for alternatives.

After this is done, we ask the person who has recorded the alternatives to share with us what has been said by the trio.

It is through this that students realize that people may think and act in the same manner, or that there are many different ways to try to resolve a problem, or that there are always possible solutions to every problem if we consider alternatives. It will also indicate to what extent a person will allow himself to become involved with other people and what feelings and ideas he is protecting.

3. *Values Voting.* This is a strategy that allows a student to indicate his feelings and thoughts publicly on any questions asked of him and to see how others feel about the same things. It emphasizes that people differ. This is a time when he can give an answer without being told that he is right or wrong. His opinion on an issue is respected. The value of this strategy in the development of self-confidence is immeasurable.

Directions: The teacher explains that a vote will be taken on 10 questions and each student will show how he feels or thinks about the subject by doing the following: positive answer—raise hands; negative answer—thumbs down; neutral or pass—fold arms.

If the student feels strongly about the subject, he may shake his hand vigorously up or down as the case may be.

All questions must begin with "How many of you." Some examples of questions are:

1. How many of you follow a religion?
2. How many of you are happy in school?
3. How many of you are honest all the time?
4. How many of you have a best friend?
5. How many of you are in favor of war?
6. How many of you choose your own clothes?
7. How many of you feel loved?
8. How many of you think sex education should be taught in school?
9. How many of you would like to live the rest of your life where you are living now?
10. How many of you think a family should be limited in size?

After the questions have been asked,

Teachers improve their rapport with each other and with pupils.

the teacher can ask several students to share their feelings about a particular question and give reasons for voting as they did. This, of course, is on a voluntary basis. This strategy is a learning experience for the teacher because he is in close contact with feelings and ideas and values that his students are revealing. It is also a form of public affirmation of what he prizes or cherishes. It is up to the teacher to incorporate these in his teaching. Those questions where big differences occur can lead to good class discussions. After the first session, students are encouraged to bring in their own questions to have the class vote on them.

4. *Continuum.* The continuum is another device to get our students to examine how they stand or feel about issues at a particular moment in time. This shows how people are the same or differ, and that there are many different positions on an issue. The position a student chooses on a continuum is not fixed. A student may change his mind due to certain experiences and reexamination of his feelings. In that case he will change his position on the continuum.

Directions: A line is drawn and two opposite ideas are put on each end of the line. Pupils take a position on this line which represents where they stand on the issue at that moment. They may not use the center—this is reserved for "compulsive moderates."

For example, if the subject is School Marks, the continuum may appear as follows:

Mable Marks_____☐_____Gradeless George

The student is told to put his mark at the place he stands on this line.

Continuum on Draft
Dodger Dan_____☐_____Eager Egbert
Continuum on Medicine
Pillbox Pauline_____☐_____Natural Nell

Students are encouraged to think about their answers and to make any changes in position they wish to at subsequent sessions. They are made to feel free to change their position as they weigh more evidence. The value here is that students may see how their peers think and feel. Sharing the same experience draws the group together and gives it the comforting feeling of not being alone. This strategy can be the forerunner of exciting discussions.

5. *Rank Order.* This strategy involves decision making, evaluating, weighing consequences, judging, in a very realistic way. The student has to become totally involved in the problem at hand because he has important choices to make.

Directions: The student is given three statements and he must choose which would be hardest for him to do or tolerate as a first choice; second choice, less hard; third choice, easiest for him to do or tolerate.

1. Three "things" that some men do that people do not like:
   a. A man who always interrupts his wife, finishes her story, contradicts her.
   b. A man who lies around watching TV all day.
   c. A man who smokes a pack of cigarettes a day.

2. You are on a Congressional Committee in Washington, D.C. $10,000,000 has been given for three worthy causes. Which would you do first, second, third? You must spend all the money on one thing.
   a. Use the money to clean up rivers, garbage, sewage, pollution.
   b. Train those who do not have jobs.
   c. Divide the money among 10,000 needy families.

3. Which would you find hardest to do?
   a. Drop a bomb on Vietnam?
   b. Electrocute a man who has been judged to die in the electric chair?
   c. Run over someone who is threatening you with harm while you are driving your car?

The valuing process weaves together critical thinking and affective education.

This strategy allows the student to compare his thinking to that of his classmates. If they feel as he does, he feels reinforced. If the thinking is different from his, he can examine the issue and reevaluate his own thinking if necessary.

A variation of this strategy is to have the students list what they think might be other types of behavior that men practice that they do not like; or to list other worthy causes on which to spend $10,000,000. Any of the Rank Order Strategies might be the takeoff point for a social studies lesson, a science lesson, or an English lesson.

The few strategies we have used for demonstration purposes are just a sample of the many that have been developed. It is through these devices that our students learn to think critically in deciding what their values are. They learn to accept them, and, at the same time, to respect and tolerate other people's values.

A Better Rapport

We have been working with the values clarification approach for only nine months, and yet we see many benefits for pupils, teachers, and administrators. Pupils have felt warmth and there has been evidence of the development of mutual trust. Students like the personal attention, the relaxation, the period of "fun," the freedom to express their ideas and feelings. Discipline problems seem to disappear. Pupils feel important and they see their teachers and administrators

as human beings with the usual "ups" and "downs" of human beings. They hear that other pupils have the same problems and confusions and conflicts that they do. They hear their ideas and thoughts being accepted without either praise or condemnation.

Teachers and administrators have experienced a better understanding and a better rapport with each other and with pupils whom they can see as fellow humans. They have shared experiences with each other and with pupils and have become more aware of each other. Teachers have many opportunities to really "listen" to each other and to pupils and to build a group feeling among themselves and pupils.

Our main problem has been to contend with "killer" statements—efforts by some pupils to put each other down by ridicule, laughter, or jeering. Since we are living in a "put-down" society where all of us find it difficult to speak openly and freely of a person's strong points, we have really had to do much thinking about how to stop this at least during class time. We are also living with a society that has had the biblical ethic that "pride goeth before a fall" ingrained in it, so that all of us think that to be proud of something will hurt us; and even if we do feel proud, we keep it to ourselves. We are working on how to handle this and have seen enough success to encourage us. "Put-down" remarks and lack of self-esteem are both very characteristic of the kind of children we are working with, and this, of course, intensifies the problem.

There are authorities who doubt that values clarification work can be done with ghetto children at all. The feeling is that until basic emotional needs are met, pupils will not be able to look at their values. We understand this point of view, but we feel we have seen enough success of the type described in the previous paragraph to continue our experimentation with enthusiasm. Perhaps we will not be able to go as far with our youngsters as we could with middle class children, but we will have begun the difficult process of getting pupils to decide for themselves what they value and take steps to live the lives they would like to live. ☐

EL 31 (3): 236-37; December 1973
© 1973 ASCD

The middle school goes beyond traditional basic skills. One school in the Bronx tries to give human relations equal status with subject matter in heterogeneous groupings.

Who Needs Human Relations?

JACK LANDMAN*

A MAJOR complaint against the junior high schools is that they are dominated by a philosophy that is too subject centered. School boards, parents, evaluators have demanded evidence of learning based upon subject centered skills. To the extent that these skills have had an impact upon society, we would have to agree that the schools have played their part well. As we look around the community, the city, the nation, we note that the position of the United States with respect to scientific and technological criteria is enviable. Our standard of living is unparalleled in the history of the world and our future, barring disaster, may be filled with even more creature comforts and labor-saving devices. However, in the field of human relations, the picture is less encouraging.

William Alexander, in his report on the middle school, has said that the approach we take must be more child centered. I agree with this wholeheartedly. When a youngster enters our school we know his standardized reading score and his standardized math score, but there is no standardized human relations index. Since the need is obvious at the present time, and since so much effort is now going into reorganizing the education of the middle school years, I would make this suggestion. The clientele best suited to a major thrust aimed at enhancing the curricular status of human relations is the volatile, effervescent, self-discovering, fast-growing, rapidly-changing, transescent middle school student!

In our school we have accepted several approaches. To begin with, our organization has heterogeneity as its top priority. Just as there is no ethnic separation, there is no intellectual stratification. Each class is the same, within narrow limits. Each class is reflective of the school community in ethnicity and in ability as measured by reading scores. This carries through in subject areas as well as homerooms, and in small groups as well as large. This organization is based upon the

* Jack Landman, Principal, I.S. 180, The Bronx, New York

feeling that the best learning situation for a middle school in which human relations are given the same status as subject matter is the heterogeneous group. Socially, the middle school has already paid a very important dividend. When students and parents attend meetings or conferences, or meet accidentally in the laundry rooms, shopping centers, or playing fields, they can talk of school comfortably, knowing there is no difference between social classes in our school.

Using the "Buddy System"

To add substance to the human relations aspects of heterogeneity, it is important that pupils accept a certain responsibility for each other's progress. In our effort to develop this concern, we use a method we call the "buddy system." In its simplest form, it places upon the buddies the responsibility of keeping each other up to date in the event of absence or lost assignments. In extension, it becomes the basis for grouping, pairing, and tutoring in the various subject instructional areas. It is also used for assisting students who are in need of help on the social level. Since these latter assignments are more sensitive in nature, they are based upon a careful assessment of the personalities and needs of the partners. Teachers frequently consult each other and the guidance staff in making these recommendations.

One of the most frequently asked questions is, "Aren't we holding bright children back?" The question arises from the conviction that the best education is that which produces the best readers, the best math students; therefore, if a bright student spends time helping others who are less gifted, it would seem to follow that he would learn more working on his own.

However, there are many educational values in the buddy system. For example, there is enrichment in the act of tutoring, of explaining. In order to tutor and to explain, a student must clarify his own thinking and improve his understanding of the subject matter. From the human standpoint, he is gaining in maturity and responsibility. He is improving his image of himself. He gains in

Photo by Michael J. Sexton

Human relations in the middle school ought to be valued as highly as subject matter.

increased understanding of the nature of cooperation, increased understanding of the learning process, and increased ability to socialize. In short, he is improving his human relations index.

What about the charge that the bright student is losing out in the opportunity to improve his subject centered skills? We are also concerned about his needs for enrichment along these lines, and among the methods we use are honor assignments, independent study contracts, community assignments, and curricular alternatives. Because of our commitment to heterogeneity, however, let me stress that these enriched assignments are open to all students.

It is too early to make claims about the effectiveness of these approaches. Appraisal by the supervisory staff shows that racial incidents in the school are almost nonexistent. Faculty and parental evaluations support this, and it is true that pupils are comfortable with each other. Even our standardized test results show satisfactory gains.

Do we suggest this approach for all middle schools? The answer is that improvement in human relations is certainly needed and the schools must help. If these procedures do not fit each local situation, they are, at the very least, a starting point for finding some that do.   □

EL 31 (3): 233-35; December 1973
© 1973 ASCD

What About "Unified Arts" in the Middle School?

RICHARD W. MEISTER*

"Unified arts" in the Madison, Wisconsin, middle schools are learner-oriented. Goals include: exploration geared to interest and ability; proficiency in skills; developing confidence as a consumer; selecting approaches to careers; and deciding about use of leisure time.

FOR two decades now, articles have been written about the middle school concept. Attention has been focused on rationale for conversion from the traditional junior high school to the middle school. Other aspects of the transition such as organizational structure, instructional programs, teaching methodologies, and in-service programs have been described in varying detail.

Since the instructional program is the feature component of a middle school, the purpose of this article is to focus on that phase through a description of the unified arts program. The term "unified arts" is defined in Madison, Wisconsin, Public Schools as consisting of the disciplines of art, home economics, industrial arts, and in some instances vocal music and physical education.

Students of grades 6, 7, and 8 participate in all aspects of the program at all grade levels. Participation is centered on a scheduled block of instructional time (about 80 minutes two or three times weekly) and a block of open laboratory time (about 80 minutes two or three times weekly). All classes are coeducational and are team taught. The program has been planned as a continuous sequential experience allowing all students to explore the three arts areas in each of three years. As a student begins to integrate the experiences from two or more arts areas, he is encouraged to make individual decisions about the laboratory space most supportive of his immediate needs.

Planning

Planning for the unified arts program emphasized two separate components: (a) instructional program development, and (b) team organization and coordination. Planning for the instructional program was initiated prior to the transition to the middle

* Richard W. Meister, Assistant Principal, West High School, Madison, Wisconsin

school organizational structure. Planning for team development was accomplished during an in-service training program before the transition of each junior high school to a middle school. The goals of the unified arts program were developed by a staff-community task force in 1968-69 and to date have continued to set the direction for the program.

These goals are:

Exploration: to provide all middle school learners with the opportunity by which they may learn through exploration geared to their own interest and ability

Skills: to encourage all middle school learners to achieve a gratifying degree of proficiency as required through self-assessment

Consumerism: to assist all middle school learners in gaining confidence in creatively consuming personal, family, and environmental resources for effective living in a changing society

Careers: to enable all middle school students to select, through exploratory experiences, future curricula directed toward occupational and career development goals

Leisure: to help the early adolescent make decisions about leisure time.

Program Characteristics

The unified arts program shares the instructional goals of the middle school: it provides for all middle school learners; it utilizes an interdisciplinary approach; and it encourages exploration in the arts areas. Exploration is defined as (a) increased learner exposure to more subject areas and the related experiences, media, and materials therein; and (b) increased learner opportunity to explore his own interests and abilities.

How then does a unified arts program differ from a separate arts program? Unified arts:

1. Claims its general title of unified arts in preference to individualized subject area titles, thus stressing the integration of knowledge

2. Synthesizes the individual art areas into a meaningful whole

3. Integrates knowledge, skills, attitudes, and values between and among the arts as well as between the arts and academics

4. Is not a course but rather a series of instructional relationships depending on both teacher and student behaviors.

Learner Outcomes

The expected learner outcomes of the unified arts program are expressed here in two forms, behaviorally and as the learner might perceive them himself.

The child will assess his self-potential and purposefully plan for its development. (I am beginning to find out what I can do and how I can improve.)

The child will show sensitivity to the aesthetic components of his environment. (I am happy with my surroundings.)

The child will utilize precaution and employ safe practices in school, home, and community participation. (I will do all my work carefully and safely.)

The child will synthesize the components and interrelationships of the total unified arts structure. (I am beginning to see how things relate to each other as in unified arts.)

The child will capitalize on his unique and useful individual strengths. (I am finding out what I can do best.)

The child will build a balance between his individuality and mass society. (I enjoy working alone as well as with other people.)

The child will use leisure to find meaning, purpose, and self-fulfillment. (I enjoy choosing how I will use my free time.)

The child will employ the skills of consumership to meet his present needs. (I am learning about making my own selections.)

The child will think through solutions to problems. (I am growing in my ability to make decisions.)

The child will relate core learnings and open-lab and independent study opportunities to personal living. (I am discovering that it is fun to learn through exploration.)

Implementation

Various strategies are used in the unified arts program. Basically the program:

1. Utilizes a block of time, a unit of students, specialized facilities, and a team of teachers representative of the arts areas

2. Requires individual teacher competencies in human relations and decision making

3. Gives teachers, and ultimately students, decision-making responsibilities as to the relationship of learning objectives to the resources of time, space, materials, and staff

4. Is taught in large, medium, and small groups, as well as providing for individualized instruction and learner self-initiation

5. Allows for a variety of team patterns involving any combination of two or more arts areas and/or arts areas directly linked to (an) academic team(s) and/or middle school goal

6. Occupies varied instructional facilities including accommodative laboratories representative of each of the arts areas, instruction and resource materials centers, large group instructional areas, and community resources

7. Utilizes multiple instructional methodologies and media

8. Promotes flexibility across arts areas so as to give total perspective to a concept.

Evaluation

Evaluation of the unified arts program is in terms of the learner. It recognizes the value of individualized evaluation in terms of progress toward the behavioral goals established for the unified arts program. It stresses individualized instruction and evaluation in terms of degree of proficiency as required by the learner himself. In addition, it involves the necessity of assessing one's self via communication with parents, peers, and teachers.

Staffing

Unified arts is taught by a team of teachers representing the arts areas. In a school of 750 students a team of six (two from each arts area) plus a teacher aide are responsible for curriculum development and implementation congruent with the program goals. A learning coordinator, one of two in the school, assists the unified arts team via weekly team meetings in accomplishing planning and organizational expectations. Staff members must have a positive attitude toward team teaching, sensitivity toward the needs of children, and a commitment to student-centered learning. The ability and desire to participate in interdisciplinary teaching are also necessary prerequisites for a functioning unified arts team.

Other factors such as facilities and scheduling are important considerations for the efficient functioning of a unified arts program; neither, however, should dictate the program. Only two of Madison's 10 unified arts programs operate from newly designed open concept facilities. A block scheduling design is utilized, giving unified arts the equivalent of one-third of the available instructional time. Planning time for teachers is also allocated within the schedule and provides for both total team and individual arts area planning.

Programs have been initiated in 10 schools over a four-year period, with approximately 7,000 students participating each year. The first group of students to have experienced the entire three-year unified arts sequence through grades 6, 7, and 8 are in grade 10 this school year. Experienced high school staff members note definite changes about the unified arts student as compared to the student of the past with a single arts exposure. The unified arts student is described as being more willing and interested in exploratory activity, more self-directed, more sensitive to his own development and needs, and generally more open to considering his or her career development process.

By having arts-related exploratory learning experiences over a three-year development growth period, and by having opportunities to make several individual decisions about these experiences, the transitional age learner should be in an advantageous position to cope with future career, leisure, and continuing education decisions. □

PART 5

Middle Schools in Action

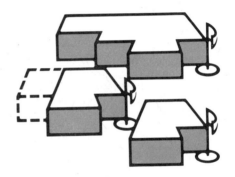

Developing trends in Florida's emerging middle schools attest to the vitality of this new movement.

EL 31 (3): 217-20; December 1973
© 1973 ASCD

The Middle School in Florida: Where Are We Now?

PAUL S. GEORGE*

THE most obvious educational accomplishment in Florida in recent years has been the rapid increase in the number of schools adopting a middle school format. Ten years ago in Florida there were fewer than ten middle schools. Today the number of schools with some combination of grades 5 through 8 is nearing 150, with a 20 percent increase in 1972; and the promise is for continued growth in numbers throughout the remainder of the decade. While this rate of growth cannot continue forever, there are already as many middle schools as junior high schools. The middle school has come to stay in Florida.

One piece of evidence that the momentum is continuing is the formation of a new Florida League of Middle Schools. The League was born in September 1972, at the Third Annual Conference of Florida Middle Schools in Tampa. The League proposes, as its overall goal, to help middle schools grow more toward what they wish to become.

The tentative purposes of the League are varied. It will attempt to facilitate continuing curriculum improvement, in-service education, school planning, and other phases of middle school education. It will serve as a clearinghouse for exchange of ideas, materials, and personnel needed for middle school development. The League will assist in developing plans for evaluation of middle schools in Florida. It will help to secure and maintain support of agencies and groups in the state interested in educational improvement. Finally, the League will represent the middle schools in professional and public discussions of educational programs and problems.

Toward this end, in the first year the League will be providing a regular newsletter to all middle school teachers. The League also will sponsor an annual conference, arrange intervisitations and referrals, and provide a voice for its members on matters of educational policy at the local, state, and national levels.

Certification Now Offered

Further evidence of the dynamism of the middle school movement in Florida comes in the form of a recognition of its uniqueness by the State Department of Education. The

* Paul S. George, Assistant Professor and Coordinator, Middle School Teacher Education, University of Florida, Gainesville

State Department has designed and now offers special certification in Middle School. It has further mandated that, by 1975, teachers in Florida's middle schools must possess that special certification. The underlying logic is that if, indeed, the middle school deserves to exist as a separate entity, then something special ought to be occurring in those schools, and teachers should have special training and certification to help it happen.

Middle school teacher education is a direct result of the birth of the special certificate. This teacher education, desperately needed if the middle school is to survive, is beginning to blossom throughout the state. Both in-service and preservice efforts are beginning to emerge.

For the first time in Florida, teachers will be able to earn an entirely new certification through in-service education. Teachers may return to the university to earn the middle school certificate, but they need not do so. Each county school system with a middle school has the option of submitting a plan outlining the manner in which their teachers will be trained. At this point, the major guidelines to counties from the State Department have been that each teacher seeking in-service middle school certification must have completed at least one year of successful full-time teaching in an identified middle school, and participate in an approved county level middle school in-service program. A wide variety of county programs are developing and, to ensure some uniformity, further guidelines to the counties will probably soon be forthcoming.

The University of Florida now offers an operational Middle School Teacher Education Program that permits entry at three levels. The first level is a one-quarter "add-on" program for undergraduate students who have already completed the requirements for either an elementary or secondary certificate and wish to complement their training with middle school specialization. This post-baccalaureate add-on block is a 16 quarter-hour individualized, competency-based program focused predominantly on field experiences. Seminars and "concept" sessions continuing throughout the term emphasize helping teachers become better team members and preparing them to deal with the growth and development needs of transescent students.

Graduate programs at the University of Florida in Middle School Education at the master's and specialist levels are now preparing enrolled students to assume positions of leadership throughout the state and nation. Team leaders, curriculum coordinators, principals, and others are preparing to facilitate the further implementation of the middle school concept. There is little doubt that this special training and certification will add a great deal of vitality to the life of the middle schools in Florida. Effective training programs are essential to the existence of the middle school here and elsewhere.

Changes in Instruction

Visits to middle schools throughout the state easily yield evidence of the positive effects of an increased statewide emphasis on actual, pervasive, lasting, school-level program changes. One of the most encouraging changes to be found is the exciting extent to which middle schools have been able to achieve a large measure of independence from the legacy of earlier organizational patterns. Apparently, just changing the name of the school seems to legitimize these declarations of independence. The "little high school" approach has been questioned, found wanting, and is on its way out in Florida. Middle school teachers in Florida have become convinced that independence and uniqueness in program are not only advisable but crucial to the educational experience of their students.

Individualized instruction as a preferred instructional strategy has found its way, in at least some form, into virtually every middle school in the state. The use of the learning stations approach is spreading rapidly, along with the use of unipacs or learning activity packages (LAP's). Commercial and quasi-commercial instructional systems based on an individualized approach (SRA, IPI, IGE, etc.) are being adopted widely. Some schools are experimenting with computer-managed instruction, which allows them to implement a "continuum of objectives" system involving specific learning objectives, and individual student diagnosis, prescription, and study. The emergence of quality programs in independent study for middle students can be spotted all over the state. Individualized, personalized instruction is achieving real momentum in Florida's middle schools as teachers begin to make it work.

Exploration seems to have been adopted as a central theme by most middle schools in Florida. Currently this involves an increasing flexibility, openness, and variety in the expressive or unified arts programs (home economics, industrial arts, art, music, etc.). It is beginning to mean more than this in many schools, as special interest enrichment programs spring up in every part of the state. Many special interest programs offer students daily involvement in an activity self-selected from a list of almost infinite variety. It is not unusual to see students in a single school involved in activities ranging from candlemaking or intramurals to exploratory foreign language studies and violin.[1]

Teachers in Florida's middle schools are paying increased attention to the affective side of the educational process. The role of

[1] For an interesting and complete description of these programs see: Joseph Bondi. *Developing Middle Schools*. New York: MSS Publications, Inc., 1972.

the teacher as effective guide, the facilitator of the personal growth of students, is assuming a greater and greater significance when teachers come together to discuss their goals and objectives. Health and sex education, a focus on the development of group process skills, increased opportunities for students to experience success, and a greater concern for the role of emotion in the classroom are just a few of the things middle school teachers seem to want to bring to their classrooms.

Almost every middle school in the state is making an effort to design a schedule and a system of grouping which fit what teachers and students want to do, rather than the reverse. In contrast to the situation a few years ago, when the inflexible six-period day existed in every school, today's middle schools are trying out a variety of scheduling patterns which they describe as block, diagonal, modular, and so forth. A number of alternatives to the traditional system of grouping strictly by chronological age are in use, with attempts at multiage grouping achieving a minimum level of popularity among those who try it.

Team Teaching

Team teaching has become a favorite form of teacher deployment in Florida's middle schools. Teachers and principals from schools where there is no authentic attempt at teaming of some kind talk as though their schools were committing a terrible sin of

Exploration seems to have been adopted as a central theme by most middle schools in Florida. Currently this involves an increasing flexibility, openness, and variety in the expressive or unified arts programs (home economics, industrial arts, art, music, etc.).

omission. Exactly what form of teaching will emerge as the most popular one 10 years from now is still unknown, but the fact that teaming itself seems here to stay is questioned by few Florida middle school educators.

Theorists and advocates of the middle school concept in universities and county level administrators and staff members are pushing what they describe as interdisciplinary team teaching. One brand of interdisciplinary teaming practiced successfully in a number of Florida middle schools has four-person teams composed of one specialist from each of the areas of language arts, social studies, science, and math. Each specialist serves as the resource person for his particular area, doing a great deal of the planning for the teaching of that subject. Each teacher on the team, however, teaches all four of the academic subjects. Advocates of this method point to a number of advantages, including the easier correlation of subject matter areas, and an increased ability of teachers to concentrate on the student first and all else second.

Other schools tend to rely on single-discipline teams, for example, the social studies team. Those who are convinced of the merits of this brand of teaming claim that it is the best way to ensure that each academic area is taught by those who know enough about it.

As changes occur with greater frequency and impact, an interesting phenomenon is taking place in Florida's middle schools. Faculties are becoming painfully aware, in some cases, that what their written philosophy says they believe and do is not obvious in the day-to-day operation of the school. The faculties of other middle schools are discovering that the goals and objectives that went down on paper five or ten years ago no longer have any relevance to or connection with their current practices. As a result, all over the state middle school faculties are making real efforts to see that there is a congruence between what the school says it believes and what happens to kids in the school. This rethinking of goals and resultant programs promises a healthier future for education for the middle years in Florida.

What Remains To Be Done

The middle school movement in Florida is a healthy, growing, enthusiastic development. Floyd Christian, Commissioner of Education in Florida, stated in September 1972 that "Florida's experiment in middle schools is probably the most successfully innovative program undertaken by the Florida Department of Education." And so it seems; but much remains to be accomplished before educators concerned with the school lives of emerging adolescents can rest easily on their laurels.

Special middle school certification in Florida has been a great boon to the movement. New efforts in this area are needed, however. The confusing number of overlapping certificates must be reduced. The presently limited middle school certificate must be expanded to allow teachers who possess it to teach in grades 5 through 8, regardless of the name on the front of the school building.

This hoped-for expansion of the middle school certificate implies an even more necessary development. The Middle School, as a concept, must come to include all schools which are intermediate, those schools between elementary and high school. Educators concerned with this area of schooling must see to it that all schools attempting to meet the needs of transescents view themselves as helpmates rather than as rivals struggling over disputed territory. A broader certification, resulting from this kind of outlook, will help to strengthen programs for transescents by prompting teacher education programs to provide the all-important training for potential faculty.

The middle school movement in Florida is a dynamic, exciting phenomenon. Almost everyone who is participating in the improvement of educational experiences for emerging adolescents in Florida seems caught up in an enthusiasm that has been missing from this part of schooling for a long time. This observer is convinced that, if this momentum continues to grow, great progress will be made in education for the middle years of school in Florida and elsewhere. □

THE CAMELOT

"I enjoyed the trip to Frost Valley because I found out that just because a person's skin color is different from yours it doesn't mean you can't have fun with him. Also, what made the trip a success was our surroundings. We were surrounded by mountains and forests."

"I learned the difference between Great Neck and J.H.S. 118. They listen to different records and they dance different, they even talk with a different accent. I think this is all because they live in a very different environment. I learned to live with people I never knew before or saw before. I learned how to be responsible in my own way."—Alfred

"I never have in my life had a lot of conversation with people about how my life has been and how different it is from small towns."—Shorty

"I had never had a chance to go climbing mountains and crossing cable bridges before."—Eddie

THESE words were the written comments of some of the 28 ninth year boys and girls in the Camelot Program of the Wm. W. Niles J.H.S. 118, Bronx, New York City, who participated in a trip to Frost Valley, New York, during the week of April 17, 1972. We were very much moved by the written and oral comments, and we were delighted by the interaction that took place between two groups of youngsters whose environment, way of life, and even language were different.

This trip may have been a "first" of an urban and suburban students' country get-together.

The Camelot Program at Niles Junior High School is an experimental program which is designed to meet the needs of 45 potential dropouts. It is a classroom without walls, which has its own curriculum essentially independent of the mainstream of the school. The purposes are to give boys and girls a flexible program which will allow them to explore, free of customary curricular restraints, areas of study in which they are interested; to progress at their own rate of speed; to develop innate talents; to relate to one another as human beings; and to assume responsibility for their actions. The taste of success, which had been an elusive thing for the past nine years for these students, is the psychological key to their future. This program has provided success for the first time for many of them during this first experimental year at the school.

Niles Junior High School is located in one of the most deprived pockets of New York City. A densely populated area, with streets littered with abandoned cars, garbage, broken bottles, bent cans, and telephone wires strung with abandoned swinging sneakers. Good people live here, struggling to bring up their children with values, morals, and dignity—good people struggling on meager salaries or on welfare, fighting to keep their

EL 30 (2): 144-48; November 1972
© 1972 ASCD

PROGRAM

MILDRED W. ABRAMOWITZ*
CLAUDIA C. MACARI

children away from the drug addicts, the pushers, the muggers, and the gangs. Sixty-five percent are of Puerto Rican background; the remainder are Black.

Working within the environment of the alternate classroom, the four teachers assigned to the program served the dual role of teachers and guidance advisors. These teachers, Eugene Scher, Richard Acosta, Susan Fauer, and Paul Bablove, are licensed in the academic areas of mathematics, social studies, Spanish, science, and English; but above all, they have qualities to which these students readily responded: warmth, interest, and dedication.

The lives of the students outside of school are circumscribed by the neighborhood they live in. They rarely go outside of these boundaries—except for occasional family trips to New Jersey, Connecticut, or to a nearby beach. The teachers have taken them to places of interest all over the city during the school day. However, when the teachers brought up the subject of a big trip away from home, the students' excitement was tremendous. When the teachers approached us with the idea, we quickly computed the cost of such a trip and were quite discouraged by the fact that it seemed to be a financial impossibility. The idea and the meaning it had for the students persisted, however, so we began to search for a solution to the problem.

An Exchange

Eight years ago an exchange was initiated between Great Neck North J.H.S.[1] and Wm. W. Niles J.H.S. Annually a group of students from each school would visit the other's school and spend two days together exchanging ideas and opinions on current issues and problems. They would visit classes, lunch together, and participate in special programs arranged for the day.

For the past few years, we had found an increasing demand for a more extensive exchange. Although there were follow-up visits on weekends, these were always difficult to effect because we did not have money for transportation costs.

When the teachers and supervisors involved met over a weekend to make the usual plans for the 1972 exchange, a unanimous desire for a week-long experience was expressed. We explored all the possibilities of such outings, but the cost of transportation seemed prohibitive. Finally, someone came up with the idea of using one bus trip to the country and staying somewhere for an entire week. This was the answer to our problem.

[1] Great Neck is just outside New York City and is a relatively affluent suburb.
* Mildred W. Abramowitz, Professor of Education, Brooklyn College, New York; and Claudia Macari, Assistant Principal, Niles Junior High School 118 Bronx, New York

Questions	Most Numerous Answers of 30 Niles Participants
1. High point for you	1. Meeting new people, pillow fights, hikes, making new friends
2. Low point for you	2. Coming home (unanimous)
3. Rank three things you liked	3. Varied response—covered all the activities
4. Rank three things you didn't like	4. Coming home, nothing, rules about getting up or going to bed
5. List three things you missed most from home	5. Parents, sibling, nothing
6. A person you met and why you liked him	6. Varied, but names of several individuals were mentioned by as many as five people for being "nice," "free-minded," "funny," "friendly"
7. How do you feel about your teachers after spending a week with them?	7. They are human beings, fun to be with
8. Three things you learned	8. Varied—"how to get along with people," "how to climb a mountain," "not all whites are bad," "not everyone looks for trouble," "people are people," "friendly people make you happy inside"
9. Did this trip help you to get along with strangers?	9. Unanimous variety of "yes" and "let's do it again"
10. How did you feel about not watching TV?	10. Unanimous "didn't miss it"

Figure 1. Student Reactions to the Camelot Program

Arrangements began to take shape for a trip to Frost Valley.[2]

From December 1971 to March 1972 there were meetings, telephone conversations, discussions, and planning. We all spent a weekend at Frost Valley to get acquainted with the terrain, the camp, and its facilities, and to block out the activities for 60 boys and girls who would spend the week there.

Our greatest problem was a financial one, but we were able to overcome that because a local department store and our school district gave us money. The students themselves held cake sales, decorated bottles and sold them, and saved their money so that they could pay part of their own expense. The Camelot teachers called parents who were reluctant to give their children permission to take a five-day trip away from home. This was particularly true for the girls. The teachers visited homes and assured parents that their children would be safe.

Bill Devlin, director of the YMCA Camp, visited both schools. He showed color slides and told students and parents what the camp was like, what activities and facilities were available. The excitement generated by all the activities and the anticipation of the trip was almost too much for the students. They were proud of their ability to raise one-fourth of the cost of the trip,[3] a little fearful of leaving their homes and families for a week, and a little uncertain about what to expect from the Great Neck students.

Finally the day came, and the students arrived with bags, cameras, playing cards, and goodies to eat on the trip. The teachers arrived with their totes, cameras, recorders, videotape machines, basketballs, and sundry items. A word must be said about the teachers at this point. All of them left behind wives or husbands and children and many personal responsibilities, and literally gave of themselves 24 hours a day. They had promised to watch over these boys and girls, so they took four-hour shifts during the night for the entire week. Many a night a teacher would spend time with a boy or girl, just sitting in front of a warm fire, and talking and listening person to person.

The Niles boys and girls arrived at Frost Valley first and waited anxiously for their companions of the week. The Great Neck group arrived and looked uneasily at the Niles group. Two separate camps formed, and this was not to be overcome for 24 hours. They were put to work unpacking and exploring the immediate grounds. Small prob-

[2] Frost Valley YMCA Camp; Bill Devlin, Director.

[3] The cost of the trip was $42, including bus fare per student.

lems arose about who was going to share a room with whom. Teachers helped to smooth things over, but the feeling of two separate groups remained.

The first day's activities involved some games, exploring, orientation, and meals. The seating arrangements at the tables were designed to mix the groups. Preplanned activities were scheduled for those who were interested. Boys and girls signed up for activities that interested them. Many activities that were not on schedule developed spontaneously. The teachers then wisely abandoned the schedule because as this began to happen, the wall between the two camps began breaking down.

One of the first things to bring them closer together was the common danger in climbing ice-slippery mountains. It was here that each would put out a helping hand to steady the other. This was the start. The real exchange took place when they returned to the dorms and sat around the fire, listening to one another and talking to one another about their lives, their plans, their parents, their school, their hopes. New ideas came forth and new worlds opened up.

Evaluating the Program

Our feeling is that the Frost Valley trip gave us an opportunity to see the achievement of some of the major goals that we had for this experimental year with our classroom without walls. We had known these boys and girls for two years before they were put into this alternate schooling project, and we had worked with a number of them in a Values Clarification class.[4] Therefore, we were in a position to notice changes when the students returned. We called them all together after their return, and we were immediately aware that many of the students seemed more articulate, more self-assured, and more satisfied to be in school.

We believe that these changes probably had been taking place gradually because of the Camelot program, but this week away

[4] See: Louis E. Raths, Merrill Harmin, and Sidney B. Simon. *Values and Teaching.* Charles E. Merrill Publishing Company, 1966.

seemed to make them blossom forth in a quantum jump. It is unusual to see these youngsters happy and enthusiastic about anything in school. They were bubbling over with excitement and pleasure. Since then they have been kissing and hugging us when they meet us in the neighborhood, and they offer signs of these feelings—walking along with us, insisting on carrying our packages and school portfolios, gossiping about their nonschool activities and plans.

We called all the teachers and pupils to the informal discussion room to talk about the trip and to answer some questions anonymously. The questions we gave them and a summary of their responses are shown in Figure 1.

The girls and boys were eager to answer all questions raised. Those slower at writing stayed after the others had gone to finish their questionnaires, even though they were not asked or even encouraged to do so. They insisted on doing so, which, in itself, was most unusual. Later, when asked by their teachers to write a short expression of their feelings about the trip for their Camelot newspaper, they did so immediately and enthusiastically. The writing was of better quality than we were used to seeing from them. We believe that our whole experience with their reaction reinforces the notion that when pupils know their feelings and want to express them—have something to say—they will express themselves far better than their usual school performance, and they are happy to do so. We witnessed a dramatic example of this.

The Exchange Week contacts continued during the months following via letters, telephone calls, and weekend visits and outings. Such activity naturally brought about communications between parents. The culmination occurred when Richard Sherman, principal of Great Neck North Junior High School, was invited to be the speaker for our graduation and the Great Neck boys and girls were also invited to come with him, to attend the ceremony, and to participate in a reception afterward so that they could meet the parents of the Niles pupils. The universal reaction of all witnesses of these events has been a genuine feeling of friendship, love, and caring despite initial fears caused by knowledge of differences in background and resources.

We would like to share with you the feelings and thoughts of the Camelot teachers and some of the parents about the week in the country. They, too, had a learning experience. One reaction follows:

There were a number of goals that we had hoped to accomplish by taking our students to Frost Valley. We wanted them to discover that they could learn outside of the traditional classroom, that learning could be an enjoyable experience, that there is a different type of life outside of the ghetto and, most important, that white children are no different from black children. I feel that we achieved every one of our goals. It would be very difficult to determine the exact degree to which we were successful, but if tears at departure were an accurate indicator, then there is no doubt that this experience was a most successful one.

It was gratifying to see young people from different ethnic and social backgrounds making an attempt to get to know each other better, to give each other a chance. These children can now be looked at by society as an example of what human relations could and should be like. —E. Scher

Our conclusion is that no amount of busing can take the place of living together for five days. The first day and a half was spent in armed cautiousness, suspicion, and fear on both sides. However, once the "ice was broken" and the students began to mix in pillow fights, eating, playing pool, hikes, and rap sessions held through the night, they learned a great deal from each other about the problems that face a democratic society, and they learned about these problems on a personal level they could understand. They were excited when talking about their own lives with someone who did not know about them. One boy said, "I never looked at my life the way I had to in answering their questions." Another said, "You really don't know a person until you share a room with him." Another, "I regret I found out how nice they were too late." A girl said, "I think it is beautiful finding out that you don't have to be a friend for a long time to be a friend." Another said, "I feel all people who don't get along are missing something."

To answer the argument that these pupils are not ready for such an experience, or that it causes discontent, or that a one-shot experience has no significance, we can only say that these generalizations were not true for the Frost Valley trip. New vistas were opened, contacts were made and continued, prejudices were shaken and questioned by experiences—all proving that much learning takes place outside the classroom. Students need experiences outside their own environment and with others different from them. There must be less talking about what to do and more doing it.

We learned that there is high performance and there are no discipline problems when pupils are learning what they regard as exciting to know.

We wonder how long it is going to take teachers to revitalize their teaching using the powerful motivating forces of attitudes and emotion in sparking learning.

We wonder when things that are entrenched in schools because they have always been there will have to prove themselves as worthy of continuance.

We wonder if going to the country together will become a regular part of the curriculum. □

EL 30 (6): 563-65; March 1973
© 1973 ASCD

Self-Instruction:
An Experimental Program

ROBERT L. CRANE
MARJORY E. JACOBSON

THE Self-Instruction Center is the name given to the location for students who participate in an experimental project at Webber Junior High School in Saginaw, Michigan. The project is formally called the Adjusted-Study Program, a title which is not particularly original. Similar programs have been tried in other school districts, for example, Forsyth Junior High School in Ann Arbor, Michigan.

Webber Junior High School has an enrollment of 1,040 students in grades 7, 8, and 9, located in a lower-middle class neighborhood in the southeastern part of Saginaw. The racial breakdown of the school's enrollment is approximately 62 percent White, 22 percent Black, and 16 percent Mexican American. This distribution resembles very closely the total racial makeup of the entire city.

Webber, like most junior high schools of its size, has a number of students experiencing behavioral as well as learning difficulties. As in many other urban settings during the past few years, the number and seriousness of these difficulties have been growing. The rate of this growth is out of proportion to increasing enrollment. Several methods, such as counseling, reprimanding, parent conferences, individualized attention from teachers, services of school social workers, and innovative remedial and enrichment-type programs have been tried to help these youngsters. These have met with varying measures of success. In spite of these efforts, many of the problems persist.

During the 1970-71 school year the curriculum committee of the building faculty spent much of its time discussing the situation and examining many programs that might be effective. After a great deal of work, the Adjusted-Study Project was developed. The program was proposed to the board of education which, after careful study, accepted and funded the project on a pilot basis for the fall of 1971.

A regular classroom was converted into a comfortable, lounge-type setting and was provided with equipment, such as study carrels, cassette recorders, filmloop projector, record player, language-master, cash register, adding machines, and a number of other items appropriate for individualized instruction.

A referral plan was developed in which a youngster experiencing academic or behavioral difficulties could be referred to the Adjusted-Study Program in the Self-Instruction Center. This could be done by his classroom teachers, counselor, or an administrator.

Student self-referral, which has been occurring more and more frequently, was another possibility. All referral applications are reviewed by a screening committee made up of counselors, teachers, and administrators who try to determine whether or not this program would be helpful to the youngster.

If a student is admitted to the program, he is scheduled from the class which is giving him most difficulty into the Self-Instruction Center for two class periods each week. Consecutive days are avoided. This is a very important aspect of the program because the referring teacher agrees to continue working with the youngster. According to the design of the program, the student remains in the classroom the remaining three days. His teacher confers with the instructor in the SIC regarding the youngster's needs and progress. The referring teacher also agrees to send academic assignments to the SIC to coordinate instruction for the student. Thus it is the responsibility of the referring teacher to continue evaluating the youngster's academic work.

With this type of program, classroom teachers have the opportunity to help youngsters stay in class rather than "get rid" of them. The program also affords teachers the opportunity to examine their own techniques and to apply successful methods used in the SIC to the logistics and instruction in their own classrooms.

Certainly the key to success in any program such as this is the careful selection of the Adjusted-Study instructor. He also must be a very patient, understanding person, with a wide knowledge of subject matter and teaching strategies and, most important, a sincere interest in helping deviant youngsters to improve their lot.

It should be pointed out that every effort has been made to secure a supportive staff to assist the instructor. Fortunately, many college students from nearby Saginaw Valley College and Delta College have offered their services as part-time tutors. The program has been primarily aided by full-time student teachers from Michigan State University. Tutors and student teachers together have complemented one another in contributing toward the development of the program.

A student must learn to accept responsibility for his own actions while in the SIC. He will be encouraged and motivated as much as possible, but in the final analysis he must take it upon himself to make an effort. Obviously, a program such as this is not going to solve all the ills of deviant youngsters. Therefore, it is to be expected that anyone considering such a program is certain to experience some difficulties; however, it appears at this point that SIC statistics will show success not only in improved attitudes and fewer antisocial behaviors but increased achievement as well. Also, there has never been a single incident in the SIC that could be considered for referral as a discipline problem.

It is our feeling that Adjusted-Study should go beyond application to deviant youngsters. If the same instructional design and techniques could be applied to our average and gifted students, undoubtedly, even greater achievement would be realized. A program which adjusts the interests and aptitudes of students to their needs would have an excellent opportunity for implementation through independent study or small-group seminars in the Self-Instruction Center.

—ROBERT L. CRANE, *Principal, Webber Junior High School, Saginaw; and* MARJORY E. JACOBSON, *Director, Central Michigan University Off Campus Education, Saginaw*

EL 30 (8): 733-35; May 1973

Big Friend:
A Tutorial Program

VERNA KEENE BAKER*

THE most effective teachers for some children, some of the time, are other children. Time, space, and personnel can make it possible for two children to work together as a team in a one-to-one relationship. An older student, nine to thirteen years of age, teams with a younger student, five to eight years of age, in order to meet the needs of one or both members of the team.

We have known for many years that children often learn games and songs from other children. We are attempting to extend this same way of learning to achieve knowledge, skills, and attitudes at home and at school.

A "Big Friend" program, which is a part of our differentiated staffing at Holmes School, has contributed successfully toward growth in self-direction and self-worth, according to testimonials of students, teachers, and parents during the past nine years.

Friends Meet

The Big Friend program began at Holmes School when a teacher expressed concern about three of his older students who lacked a feeling of self-worth. One student was much overweight, one an epileptic, while another needed opportunities for a wide variety of experiences which he could select and direct. Approaches that might help these children were discussed. Finally, through combined efforts of the staff, we agreed that these students might develop more confidence if they participated in experiences requiring their own direction and leadership.

Each of the three older students was teamed with a younger student. Each teacher predicted social and academic benefits for the child involved in one-to-one relationship experiences.

Two of the three teams continued to operate, but one member of a team wanted to quit because he said, "My little friend won't do what I want him to do."

The relationship of Big Friend to Little Friend provides the younger child with someone of his very own to help him with his problems. It also helps the older pupil who assumes responsibility for assisting the younger member of the team.

Value of the Program

The Big Friend program has mushroomed from three teams to more than 60 teams at present. When a teacher identifies a child (older or younger) who might benefit from a one-to-one learning experience, he contacts the director of the program.

* Verna Keene Baker, Principal, Holmes School, Mesa, Arizona

Both children benefit from a one-to-one learning experience.

The program director is a teacher who applies for this role each spring and who must be accepted by the School Council. The director works with all teachers to compile two lists, one of younger students who need help and one of older students whose identified needs might be met in a team arrangement.

Other tasks of the director are to:

1. Consult with teachers about matching a Big Friend with a Little Friend

2. Prepare a written schedule of times when teams may work

3. Arrange for space where teams will work

4. Meet with Big Friends and explain: (a) time they will meet with their Little Friends, (b) teaching materials they will use, and (c) methods they might use to help their Little Friends achieve their tasks

5. Prepare a paper including: (a) name and room number of Little Friend, (b) name and room number of Big Friend, (c) time for the older student to call for and then return the Little Friend to his room, and (d) a list of skills with which the younger child may need help

6. Conduct sessions with the older students about: (a) displaying and explaining uses of new materials, (b) discussions with Little Friends, (c) making materials, and (d) problems of their partners.

The Big Friend goes to his Little Friend's classroom and escorts him to their assigned work space. At present the location for most teams is the dining room, where there are 40 round tables to accommodate as many as 40 teams, each half hour, every morning from 8:30 until 11:00. The younger child's teacher assumes responsibility for the work or play activities to take place during the half hour. For example, a six-year-old student who needs help with printing may have his Big Friend's assistance for 30 minutes.

Often, when help is not immediately available from the teacher, a child may even forget what he wanted to know. Sometimes this results in negative behaviors requiring even more of the teacher's time. At Holmes School, a Big Friend may be able to supply this immediate attention.

The younger child's interests may be more fully developed by a Big Friend who has similar interests. Another benefit of the program is in decision making, which begins when a student decides whether he wants to work on a team and continues until he chooses to stop working on a team.

An Aide Contributes, Too

An aide for the Big Friend program is available to answer student questions. At first, children seemed to resent an aide, saying they could direct themselves. We explained that the aide was to assist them only if they asked for help. We agreed that under ordinary circumstances they could direct themselves very well.

Each morning the aide loads a cart with a variety of resources children may use after completing assigned tasks. The aide also: assists children in obtaining games, answers questions about their work tasks, prepares resources, types and binds books children have written, prepares flannel board stories, and makes and files dittos.

One advantage common to older children is the gaining of insight into their own problems as they help younger children: use microscopes, match numerals, make items for bulletin boards, work on art projects, read together, look at slides, use the telephone, practice handwriting skills, listen to stories, use individual filmstrip projectors, work math problems, play with reading games, play with math games, or use manipulative objects so as to understand math better.

As the Big Friend directs another individual, he becomes more skillful in directing himself. A Big Friend who helps a younger child with motor coordination exercises is referred to as "coach."

Involvement in this program offers a wide variety of opportunities for changes in behavior. An older child who learns slowly and feels uncomfortable in group situations may feel challenged and become more sensitive when he learns that even a younger friend needs to work slowly. Young children who have problems at home or at school often function more comfortably knowing they will be with their friends every day.

Students Respond

Teachers and the director encourage students to ask for conferences, and teachers call students together to evaluate their team experiences. Some actual comments of the children from these meetings are: "I get more attention," "I'm a better reader, writer, and I'm good in arithmetic," "It helped me understand smaller children," "I'm happy I am one

When the teacher is busy, an older student may supply immediate attention.

The younger child's interests are shared by a Big Friend.

of the lucky ones who has the chance to tutor," "I get to where I can associate with people," "When I read her stories it helps me in reading," "It makes me think more and makes me think ahead," "A tutor has more experiences with people," "I'm not nearly as shy."

The older student is challenged to complete his own tasks, and to organize his time so he may have the half hour with his Little Friend. Serving unselfishly, the Big Friend grows in his ability and desire to help others. Other values developed are:

1. *Leadership*—the Big Friend is responsible for his Little Friend and is a model in behavior and attitudes.

2. *Initiative*—the Big Friend prepares materials and plans activities.

3. *Self-direction*—as the Big Friend directs another individual, he becomes more capable of directing himself.

4. *Study habits*—the Big Friend organizes his time so he can help his Little Friend for 30 minutes.

5. *Unselfishness*—the Big Friend's efforts are directed toward his Little Friend's interests and needs.

6. *Opportunity for success and development of self-worth*—an older, slower student who has difficulty achieving success finds ways to help his Little Friend feel successful.   ☐

EL 32 (6): 421-23 March 1975
© 1975 ASCD

Middle School Research 1968-1974:
A Review of Substantial Studies

JON W. WILES
JULIA THOMASON

Findings indicate little evidence by which to evaluate middle school education. A systematic approach emphasizing qualities distinctive to middle school education is greatly needed.

AFTER nearly a decade of existence, the middle school has firmly established itself as a legitimate and acceptable model of intermediate education in America. While exact figures are unavailable due to the rapid growth of middle schools, somewhere between one-third and one-half of all intermediate schools in the United States now bear this label.

During the past six years, research studies have sought to evaluate the effectiveness of the middle school according to a variety of criteria. Most such research has been comparative in nature, as it should be, assessing the merits of the middle school in relation to other forms of intermediate education.

The purpose of the present review of middle school research was to identify and summarize studies of substance which sought to evaluate middle schools in a systematic way. Particular emphasis was given to comparative studies, and the search was restricted to sources readily available in the literature. A total of 27 studies were reviewed, of which 13 were found to be substantial in terms of research design, number of subjects assessed, and usable findings.

Research Limitations

Existing research on middle school education is of remarkably low quality. Most of the studies to date have been either the result of dissertation work or studies by junior high and middle school advocates. For this reason alone, the objectivity of such studies is questionable. This review utilizes seven dissertation studies and six school-sponsored research studies.

Another problem with existing research is that it comes from a limited number of states and regions of the country. Most of the existing middle school research has been done in Florida, New York, Pennsylvania, and Michigan, although this review utilizes studies from a total of seven states.

Finally, most existing research on the middle school has been concerned with only four areas: academic achievement, attitudes, self-concepts, and facilities. While these areas of concern will serve as organizers for providing a summary, it appears that other equally important questions have been ignored by researchers.

In particular, the studies reviewed were limited in value because they did not precisely define middle schools, because they did not consider how long such schools had been in existence, because they did not indicate how long pupils in such schools had experienced the middle school program, and because they did not indicate the reason for the establishment of such schools. All of these factors, we believe, would significantly affect the findings.

Research Findings

The findings of the studies below are limited to the category in which they are listed. Nearly all of the studies cited looked at other categories and had other findings as well as those mentioned.

Achievement—Six studies were found which looked at academic achievement in middle schools and compared such achievement to other forms of intermediate education. Most of the studies were based on national standardized tests. Three studies (Eholich and Murray, 1969; Glissmeyer, 1969; and Mooney, 1970) found no significant differences in achievement for middle schoolers when compared to equivalent students in other forms of intermediate education. One study (Trauschke, 1970) indicated more achievement for middle school students, but only after at least two years of treatment in middle schools. Two studies (Howell, 1969; and Case, 1970) found middle school pupils achieving higher in some academic areas than their counterparts in other forms of intermediate education.

Attitudes—Two kinds of attitudes were addressed by the studies reviewed: attitudes of students toward school and attitudes of parents and teachers toward the middle school program. Two studies (Eholich and Murray, 1969; and Wood, 1973) found no significant differences in student attitudes toward school. Three studies (Elie, 1970; Schoo, 1970; and Bryan and Erickson, 1970) found a significant difference in the positive attitudes middle schoolers had toward school. The Elie study also revealed a greater con-

cern of middle school students with social and emotional questions.

Three studies (Howell, 1969; Trauschke, 1970; and Bryan and Erickson, 1970) found a significant difference in the positive attitudes of classroom teachers toward school in middle schools. The Bryan and Erickson study also found an increase in favorable attitude among parents toward the middle school program.

Self-Concept—In the area of self-concept and self-perception among students, four studies (Case, 1970; Eholich and Murray, 1969; Elie, 1970; and Trauschke, 1970) found no significant difference between middle school students and control students studied, while two studies (Schoo, 1970; and Soares, Soares, and Pumerantz, 1973) found middle school students having significantly *lowered* self-concepts when compared to students in other forms of intermediate education.

Facilities—Two studies (Davis, 1970; and Gatewood, 1970) looked at facilities in middle schools and other forms of intermediate education and found no significant differences.

Other Findings

The review of other studies on the middle school revealed some findings worthy of mention. A study by Krinsky and Pumerantz details that little is being done at present to prepare middle school teachers in colleges and universities. A study by Bough, McClure, and Sinks documents that less than one-fourth of middle schools in the midwest are including the fifth grade in middle schools despite the human growth and development rationale of the middle school. Other studies (Howell, 1969; and Mooney, 1970) indicate that middle schools have increased attendance and (Howell) lowered discipline problems.

After nearly ten years of existence, there is little evidence available by which to evaluate the merits of middle school education. This condition, however, is not unique to middle schools. Poor research procedures, a narrow and biased focus, and the failure to clearly define the subject of study have contributed to this condition.

There is need for a systematic study of middle school education, emphasizing those qualities which are distinctive to middle school education. Particularly needed, at this time, is a method of identifying middle schools which, in their practices, follow the guidelines of the middle school literature.

References

M. Bough, J. McClure, and T. Sinks. "The Middle School—A Five State Survey." *Clearing House* 47 (3): 162-66; November 1972.

C. Bryan and E. Erickson. "Structural Effects on School Behavior: A Comparison of Middle School and Junior High School Programs." Grand Rapids, Michigan: Grand Rapids Public Schools, June 1970.

D. Case. "A Comparative Study of Fifth Graders in a New Middle School with Fifth Graders in Elementary Self-Contained Classrooms." Doctoral dissertation. Gainesville: University of Florida, 1970.

E. Davis. "A Comparative Study of Middle Schools and Junior High Schools in New York State." Doctoral dissertation. Albuquerque: University of New Mexico, 1970.

V. Eholich and K. Murray. "New Curriculum Activities in the Pilot Intermediate Schools of New York City." New York: Center for Urban Education, October 1969.

M. Elie. "A Comparative Study of Middle School and Junior High School Students in Terms of Socio-Emotional Problems, Self-Concept, Ability To Learn, Creative Thinking Ability, and Physical Fitness and Health." Doctoral dissertation. East Lansing: Michigan State University, 1970.

T. Gatewood. "A Comparative Study of the Functions, Organizational Structure, and Instructional Process of Selected Junior High Schools and Selected Middle Schools." Doctoral dissertation. Bloomington: Indiana University, 1970.

C. Glissmeyer. "Which School for the Sixth Grader: The Elementary or the Middle School?" *California Journal of Educational Research* 20 (4): 176-85; September 1969.

B. Howell. "The Middle School, Is It Really Any Better?" *The North Central Association Quarterly* 43 (3): 43-44; Winter 1969.

J. Krinsky and P. Pumerantz. "Middle School Teacher Preparation Programs." *Journal of Teacher Education* 23 (4): 468-70; Winter 1972.

P. Mooney. "A Comparative Study of Achievement and Attendance of 10-14-Year-Olds in a Middle School and in Other School Organizations." Doctoral dissertation. Gainesville: University of Florida, 1970.

P. Schoo. "Students' Self-Concept, Social Behavior, and Attitudes Toward School in Middle and Junior High Schools." Doctoral dissertation. Ann Arbor: University of Michigan, 1970.

L. Soares, A. Soares, and P. Pumerantz. "Self-Perceptions of Middle School Pupils." *Elementary School Journal* 73 (7): 381-89; April 1973.

E. Trauschke. "An Evaluation of a Middle School by a Comparison of the Achievement, Attitudes, and Self-Concept of Students in a Middle School with Students in Other School Organizations." Doctoral dissertation. Gainesville: University of Florida, 1970.

F. Wood. "A Comparison of Student Attitudes in Junior High and Middle Schools." *High School Journal* 56 (8): 355-61; May 1973.

—JON W. WILES, *Assistant Professor of Education and* JULIA THOMASON, *Doctoral student; both at George Peabody College for Teachers, Nashville, Tennessee.*

Contributors

Mildred W. Abramowitz

William M. Alexander

Verna Keene Baker

Grover H. Baldwin

Donald E. Barnes

Wilma W. Bidwell

Joseph C. Bondi, Jr.

Mary F. Compton

Robert L. Crane

Thomas E. Curtis

Jack A. DeVelbiss

James DiVirgilio

Donald H. Eichhorn

Dorothy L. Fisher

Thomas E. Gatewood

Paul S. George

Nicholas P. Georgiady

Philip J. Harvey

Marjory E. Jacobson

Mauritz Johnson, Jr.

Jack Landman

John Lavender

Robert R. Leeper

Claudia C. Macari

Richard W. Meister

Wanda B. Mitchell

Patrick F. Mooney

Norman G. Olson

Louis G. Romano

Charles E. Skipper

Charlotte Ann Springfield

Julia Thomason

Michael F. Tobin

Conrad F. Toepfer, Jr.

E. M. Trauschke

William W. Wattenberg

Jon W. Wiles

ASCD Publications, Winter 1975

Yearbooks

Balance in the Curriculum (610-17274)	$5.00
Education for an Open Society (610-74012)	$8.00
Education for Peace: Focus on Mankind (610-17946)	$7.50
Evaluation as Feedback and Guide (610-17700)	$6.50
Freedom, Bureaucracy, & Schooling (610-17508)	$6.50
Leadership for Improving Instruction (610-17454)	$4.00
Learning and Mental Health in the School (610-17674)	$5.00
Life Skills in School and Society (610-17786)	$5.50
A New Look at Progressive Education (610-17812)	$8.00
Schools in Search of Meaning (610-75044)	$8.50
Perceiving, Behaving, Becoming: A New Focus for Education (610-17278)	$5.00
To Nurture Humaneness: Commitment for the '70's (610-17810)	$6.00

Books and Booklets

Action Learning: Student Community Service Projects (611-74018)	$2.50
Beyond Jencks: The Myth of Equal Schooling (611-17928)	$2.00
The Changing Curriculum: Mathematics (611-17724)	$2.00
Criteria for Theories of Instruction (611-17756)	$2.00
Curricular Concerns in a Revolutionary Era (611-17852)	$6.00
Curriculum Change: Direction and Process (611-17698)	$2.00
Curriculum Materials 1974 (611-74014)	$2.00
Differentiated Staffing (611-17924)	$3.50
Discipline for Today's Children and Youth (611-17314)	$1.50
Early Childhood Education Today (611-17766)	$2.00
Educational Accountability: Beyond Behavioral Objectives (611-17856)	$2.50
Elementary School Mathematics: A Guide to Current Research (611-75056)	$5.00
Elementary School Science: A Guide to Current Research (611-17726)	$2.25
Eliminating Ethnic Bias in Instructional Materials: Comment and Bibliography (611-74020)	$3.25
Emerging Moral Dimensions in Society: Implications for Schooling (611-75052)	$3.75
Ethnic Modification of Curriculum (611-17832)	$1.00
The Humanities and the Curriculum (611-17708)	$2.00
Humanizing the Secondary School (611-17780)	$2.75
Impact of Decentralization on Curriculum: Selected Viewpoints (611-75050)	$3.75
Improving Educational Assessment & An Inventory of Measures of Affective Behavior (611-17804)	$4.50
International Dimension of Education (611-17816)	$2.25
Interpreting Language Arts Research for the Teacher (611-17846)	$4.00
Learning More About Learning (611-17310)	$2.00
Linguistics and the Classroom Teacher (611-17720)	$2.75
A Man for Tomorrow's World (611-17838)	$2.25
Middle School in the Making (611-74024)	$5.00
The Middle School We Need (611-75060)	$2.50
Needs Assessment: A Focus for Curriculum Development (611-75048)	$4.00
Observational Methods in the Classroom (611-17948)	$3.50
Open Education: Critique and Assessment (611-75054)	$4.75
Open Schools for Children (611-17916)	$3.75
Personalized Supervision (611-17680)	$1.75
Professional Supervision for Professional Teachers (611-75046)	$4.50
Removing Barriers to Humaneness in the High School (611-17848)	$2.50
Reschooling Society: A Conceptual Model (611-17950)	$2.00
The School of the Future—NOW (611-17920)	$3.75
Schools Become Accountable: A PACT Approach (611-74016)	$3.50
Social Studies for the Evolving Individual (611-17952)	$3.00
Strategy for Curriculum Change (611-17666)	$2.00
Supervision: Emerging Profession (611-17796)	$5.00
Supervision in a New Key (611-17926)	$2.50
Supervision: Perspectives and Propositions (611-17732)	$2.00
The Unstudied Curriculum: Its Impact on Children (611-17820)	$2.75
What Are the Sources of the Curriculum? (611-17522)	$1.50
Vitalizing the High School (611-74026)	$3.50
Developmental Characteristics of Children and Youth (wall chart) (611-75058)	$2.00

Discounts on quantity orders of same title to single address: 10-49 copies, 10%; 50 or more copies, 15%. Make checks or money orders payable to ASCD. Orders totaling $10.00 or less must be prepaid. Orders from institutions and businesses must be on official purchase order form. Shipping and handling charges will be added to billed purchase orders. **Please be sure to list the stock number of each publication, shown in parentheses.**

Subscription to **Educational Leadership**—$10.00 a year. ASCD Membership dues: Regular (subscription and yearbook)—$25.00 a year; Comprehensive (includes subscription and yearbook plus other books and booklets distributed during period of membership)—$35.00 a year.

Order from: **Association for Supervision and Curriculum Development**
Suite 1100, 1701 K Street, N.W., Washington, D.C. 20006